STUDENT LEADERS START HERE

ASSESSMENTS & TOOLS TO HELP YOU GROW AS A LEADER

BY DOUG FRANKLIN

HELPING YOUTH WORKERS
MAKE DISCIPLES & DEVELOP LEADERS

Published by LeaderTreks
25W560 Geneva Road, Suite 30, Carol Stream, IL 60188

Printed in the United States of America

ISBN # 978-1-934577-88-2
www.leadertreks.org
877-502-0699

TABLE **OF** CONTENTS

INTRODUCTION

What is *Student Leaders Start Here?*

Student Leaders Start Here is a practical workbook focusing on three topics that make up the starting point for developing as a leader. The process of leadership development is different for each person, but the three principles presented in the following pages are foundational to getting the right start.

To get the right start in leadership, you must understand these three key principles:

Leadership Design

Your leadership foundation is built on who you are. Each person will lead differently based on how they were created and how they have been specifically gifted by God. This information will determine how we act in different situations and allows us to serve others through our strengths.

Balancing Act

We all know a great visionary who has acted inappropriately. We also know a leader who wants everything done right but can't execute the vision. The key here is balance. A leader must learn how to execute skills, but also be someone of great character.

Mission First: People Always

God has given us a mission and the mission is people. Leaders generally value either their goals or their people, neglecting the one they do not value. But in leadership, tasks and relationships are tied together. Great leaders understand this and work hard to care for people while still reaching their goals.

Who is This Book For?

This workbook is for students who are stepping into leadership. If you are a student seeking to improve your leadership, *Student Leaders Start Here* will give you the tools you need. Leadership can be learned and you are taking the right first steps by seeking to develop your leadership at a young age. The knowledge and experience you will gain from going through this workbook will serve you for the rest of your life. As a student leader, the impact you can have is great. After all, youth ministry is not the church's ministry to students. Youth ministry is students' ministry to the world. How will you lead this ministry?

How to Use This Book

Student Leaders Start Here serves as a multi-faceted resource. In it you will find three sections, each dedicated to the foundational leadership principles you read about above. Each section or chapter will give you a thorough understanding of the principle, as well as multiple experiences for you to go through to better understand the principle in your own leadership. Since *Student Leaders Start Here* was made as a workbook, feel free to write in the book as much as you want.

Leadership Profile

On page 92 is a leadership profile for you to begin building for yourself as you complete the assessments and growth plans in each chapter. This profile will show who you are as you stand at the starting line: your strengths, areas of improvement, and an action plan for you to grow stronger as a leader.

Whatever you do, make sure you are sharing your results with someone you trust who can keep you accountable to what you are learning. Learning about your own individual leadership is never enough; it must be applied. If you share your results and thoughts about what you are learning with others, they can keep you accountable to applying your leadership.

How to Use This Book in a Small Group

Student Leaders Start Here is a great resource to use in a small group of students all seeking to improve their leadership together. A group setting allows students to challenge each other and hold each other accountable as they start their leadership journey.

At the end of each session, there are some group pages with discussion questions and a schedule for you to take a group through.

Start Here

If you're a professional runner, the preparation for a big race can be exhausting. Sunrise sprints, blistered feet, torn muscles, and a wind-burnt face could be your routine for months. There are probably days your body or you're mind want to quit on you, yet you press on because you know that, at the race's end, only one runner gets the prize.

To most onlookers, the pain you endure doesn't seem worth it. They can't fathom why anyone would willingly suffer the way you are, practice the long hours you do, or keep going in the face of failure. They just don't get it. Naysayers and skeptics don't understand your willingness to go through the struggle because they have never experienced the sweet taste of victory at the race's end. But for you, the mere thought of winning the prize impels you to train, driving you through your limitations so that you may stand at the starting line, ready to run the race.

It's the same in leadership. Great leaders have trained themselves, honing their skills and sinking the roots of their character deep into the ground. Leadership involves so many things: communication, mission, vision, relationships, honesty, and perseverance. In order to stand at the starting line as a leader, you must first train yourself for the race.

Student Leaders Start Here is a training tool that will to hone your leadership skills and give you the knowledge you need to start the race with confidence.

LEADERSHIP DESIGN

EACH RUNNER that steps up to the starting line knows how they are wired. They know if they are designed for endurance running or quick sprints. They know how to time their breaths with a stride that will sustain them to the finish line. They know where the limit is and when they have a second wind to give. As you stand at the starting line of your leadership potential, you must also know how you are wired and gifted. We call this your leadership design. These two components are different, but both vital to understand when stepping into leadership.

Wiring: The unique way God has put you together with a combination of different strengths, abilities, talents, and personality traits.

Everyone is created with certain innate qualities that make them totally original. You were created by God, hard wired with talents and personality traits that are unique to just you. No one else in the world has the same strengths you do because God created all of us individually. God has put much time into creating you and he specifically designed you with a purpose. In the book of Psalms, David writes:

> you created my inmost being; you knit me together in my mother's womb. I praise you because I am fearfully and wonderfully made; your works are wonderful, I know that full well. My frame was not hidden from you when I was made in the secret place, when I was woven together in the depths of the earth. Your eyes saw my unformed body; all the days ordained for me were written in your book before one of them came to be.
> – Psalm 139:13–16

King David, the author of this psalm, saw the truth of our wiring, realizing it was God who had made us and placed in us certain abilities and strengths. As you grow in age and wisdom, this wiring makes itself more and more clear in your life. Everyone is wired differently and brings different strengths into their leadership; God has given us the ability to grow in these areas if we put hard work into using them and challenging ourselves on a regular basis.

Gifting: The spiritual gifts that God has infused in you, equipping you for Kingdom work.

Just as it is important to know how you are wired, an understanding of how Christ has gifted you is vital. When you become a Christ-follower and the Holy Spirit comes upon you, God blesses you with spiritual gifts. These gifts are given to you for the good of advancing the Kingdom of Heaven. In his first letter to the Corinthians, Paul wrote that:

> There are different kinds of gifts, but the same Spirit distributes them. There are different kinds of service, but the same Lord. There are different kinds of working, but in all of them and in everyone it is the same God at work. Now to each one the manifestation of the Spirit is given for the common good.
> – 1 Corinthians 12:4–7

Each Christ-follower is infused with certain, unique spiritual gifts for the common good. These gifts may look similar to talents or strengths, but are not to be treated the same way. Growing in your spiritual gifts does not come from your efforts alone, but instead comes out of a deepening relationship with Christ. As your relationship with God grows and matures, your abilities within your gifts will grow.

God has built the foundation of your leadership on who you are. Each person will lead differently based on their giftedness and wiring, so knowing exactly how God has enabled you for leadership is vital. This information will determine how you act in different situations and allow you to serve others through your leadership design.

The Bible on Leadership Design

Below is a case study on the leadership design of Moses. Take some time to read through how he was uniquely created to lead the people of Israel, but also how he was intentionally gifted by God in a situation where he could not have succeeded without his help. Moses' leadership design is a direct result of God's presence in his life.

Moses' Wiring

You probably know the story of Moses leading God's people out of the Egypt. God used Moses in a powerful way as a leader. But long before the burning bush and the confrontations with Pharaoh, Moses learned how he was wired. He was a "mover" in God's Kingdom. He couldn't stand injustice and quickly became the mover that brought change to people. Unfortunately, he had some growing to do in that area before he would be equipped to lead the Israelites out of Egypt. Take a look at this...

One day, after Moses had grown up, he went out to where his own people were and watched them at their hard labor. He saw an Egyptian beating a Hebrew, one of his own people. Looking this way and that and seeing no one, he killed the Egyptian and hid him in the sand...When Pharaoh heard of this, he tried to kill Moses, but Moses fled from Pharaoh and went to live in Midian, where he sat down by a well. Now a priest of Midian had seven daughters, and they came to draw water and fill the troughs to water their father's flock. Some shepherds came along and drove them away, but Moses got up and came to their rescue and watered their flock. When the girls returned to Reuel their father, he asked them, "Why have you returned so early today?"

They answered, "An Egyptian rescued us from the shepherds. He even drew water for us and watered the flock."

"And where is he?" Reuel asked his daughters. "Why did you leave him? Invite him to have something to eat."

Moses agreed to stay with the man, who gave his daughter Zipporah to Moses in marriage. Zipporah gave birth to a son, and Moses named him Gershom, saying, "I have become a foreigner in a foreign land."
— *Exodus 2:11–12, 15–22*

God's special, unique wiring of Moses stands out clearly. Moses obviously has a strong desire for justice woven into him, as seen by his defense of not only the Hebrew slave, but also the Midianite women at the well. In both situations Moses' desire for justice compels him to create movement and make change. But in the first scenario, he went too far.

A warning to us all: We can either use our strengths or abuse our strengths as leaders; the choice is ours. We must always consider our wiring in light of God's mission, not our own. Just because we are good at something doesn't mean it's a good thing to do.

Over time, Moses grew in his strengths and eventually committed himself to living out the mission God had wired him for from day one: leading God's people out of slavery and into the Promised Land. Moses wasn't ready for that mission in his early days. But every time Moses was faced with an opportunity to be a mover and make change, he grew in this ability.

The amazing thing about God is his desire to not only meet us where we are at, using the strengths and talents he put in us, but also to equip us specifically for our mission.

Moses' Gifts

After 40 years of living in Midian, God decided it was time to bring Moses back to Egypt and use him to free the Hebrew people. You know the story…Moses encounters the burning bush and the angel of the Lord starts laying the plan out for him. The Israelites have endured extreme persecution, and God is going to deliver them through Moses, rescuing them from their oppressors and leading them into the Promised Land.

Seems perfect doesn't it? Moses hates injustice. Moses is an Israelite, yet grew up surrounded by Egyptian palace life. And Moses is a mover. It seems like he had been wired for this exact moment. Moses, however, does not believe his own strengths are enough, nor does he believe God could ever gift him in such a way to lead God's people. Over and over again Moses protests God's decision to use him in such a way.

But Moses said to God, "Who am I, that I should go to Pharaoh and bring the Israelites out of Egypt?"
— *Exodus 3:11*

Moses said to God, "Suppose I go to the Israelites and say to them, 'The God of your fathers has sent me to you,' and they ask me, 'What is his name?' Then what shall I tell them?"
— Exodus 3:13

Moses answered, "What if they do not believe me or listen to me and say, 'The Lord did not appear to you'?" — Exodus 4:1

Moses said to the Lord, "Pardon your servant, Lord. I have never been eloquent, neither in the past nor since you have spoken to your servant. I am slow of speech and tongue."
— Exodus 4:10

But Moses said, "Pardon your servant, Lord. please send someone else."
— Exodus 4:13

When looking at these verses, it's crazy that God still chose Moses to lead his people out of captivity. Moses clearly does not want to go where God is calling him, yet all of his excuses for not going are based on his own limitations. Moses does not for a moment consider that God could empower him in all the areas he is afraid. But for each excuse, God responds by gifting Moses, supplying him with what he needs to overcome every obstacle.

And God said, "I will be with you. And this will be the sign to you that it is I who have sent you: When you have brought the people out of Egypt, you will worship God on this mountain."
— Exodus 3:12

God also said to Moses, "Say this to the Israelites, 'The Lord, the God of your fathers — the God of Abraham, the God of Isaac, and the God of Jacob — has sent me to you. This is my name forever, the name you shall call me from generation to generation."
— Exodus 3:15

... The Lord said, "Throw [your staff] on the ground." Moses threw it on the ground and it became a snake, and he ran from it. Then the Lord said to him, "Reach out your hand and take it by the tail." So Moses reached out and took hold of the snake and it turned back into a staff in his hand. "This," said the Lord, "is so that they may believe that the Lord, the God of their fathers — the God of Abraham, the God of Isaac and the God of Jacob — has appeared to you."
— Exodus 4:3–5

The Lord said to him, "Who gave human beings their mouths? Who makes them deaf or mute? Who gives them sight or makes them blind? Is it not I, the Lord? Now go; I will help you speak and will teach you what to say."
— Exodus 4:11–12

Then the Lord's anger burned against Moses and he said, "What about your brother, Aaron the Levite? I know he can speak well. He is already on his way to meet you, and he will be glad to see you. You shall speak to him and put words in his mouth; I will help both of you speak and will teach you what to do. He will speak to the people for you, and it will be as if he were your mouth and as if you were God to him."
— Exodus 4:14–16

For every excuse Moses offers, God responds by supplying him with the way to triumph. Moses does not believe he is able to lead the people; God disagrees and gives him the gift of leadership. Moses doesn't think the people of Israel will believe him and God gives him words and the authority of a prophet. Moses seems stunted by his inability to speak and God sees fit to give him the gift of speaking and even sends Aaron to assist him in this endeavor until he gains more confidence.

God uses both the unique wiring of Moses and a set of gifts to accomplish his mission of freeing the Israelites. Moses was designed for leadership and so are you.

Your Leadership Design

Leadership Wiring Assessment

You were created in a specific way. There is no question that you are unique; no one has ever been exactly like you. And this special design was meant to bring about a special purpose. When you are learning about and stepping into leadership, it is vital to know how you are wired so you can lead from your strengths and talents. Since each person is an individual, everyone leads differently. At LeaderTreks, we have developed the Leadership Wiring Assessment to assist in the discovery of your leadership design.

There are four main types of leadership wiring. As you saw with Moses, he was a Mover. Each type is vital and important in a ministry. They all bring their own strengths and weaknesses. This tool will help you identify how you are wired as a leader. You will be a better team leader and team member when you become aware of your leadership wiring and recognize the leadership wiring of others.

Scoring Instructions

Following are ten statements. Complete each statement by selecting the answer that best describes you. Don't worry if your answers seem inconsistent. Treat each statement as a unique situation. Select only one response for each statement. Mark the box on the right to indicate your answer.

1. When I'm a part of a work group...

a. I would rather focus on getting the work done

b. I would rather be responsible for planning and problem-solving

c. I would rather focus on relationships

d. I would rather be responsible for the team as a whole

1.
☐ a
☐ b
☐ c
☐ d

2. I am the kind of person who prefers...

a. Getting to know the other people on a project

b. Getting other people to work on a project

c. Working on each step of a project

d. Planning a project

2.
☐ a
☐ b
☐ c
☐ d

3. People sometimes tell me that I am...

a. Good at thinking ahead

b. Good at organizing things

c. Good at taking charge

d. Good at listening and befriending

3.
☐ a
☐ b
☐ c
☐ d

4. When helping with a long and boring task...

a. I would tend to make sure everyone was involved and helping

b. I would tend to talk with others as we worked

c. I would tend to think about other ways to do our work

d. I would tend to pitch in right away and do my part

4.
☐ a
☐ b
☐ c
☐ d

5. I like it when other people...

a. Tell me I'm doing good work

b. Tell me I'm creative

c. Tell me I know how to make things happen

d. Tell me they appreciate me as a person

5.
☐ a
☐ b
☐ c
☐ d

6. When I encounter a problem or obstacle, I like to...

a. Bring others together to work it out

b. Take quick action and see what happens

c. Talk it through with another person for clarity

d. Take some time to think about it and generate options

6.
☐ a
☐ b
☐ c
☐ d

7. I consider myself to be more...

a. Idea oriented

b. People oriented

c. Task oriented

d. Goal oriented

7.
☐ a
☐ b
☐ c
☐ d

8. Other people have told me I tend to be good at...

a. Completing projects

b. Being in charge

c. Coming up with new ideas

d. Meeting new people

8.
☐ a
☐ b
☐ c
☐ d

9. What bothers me is when...	9.
a. People aren't friendly	☐ a
b. People don't finish their work	☐ b
c. People won't take risks	☐ c
d. People don't use their head	☐ d
10. Here is the most important outcome to me...	**10.**
a. I just want the team to win or reach the goal	☐ a
b. I just want team members to grow	☐ b
c. I just want teammates to get along	☐ c
d. I just want the team to get it right	☐ d

Response Sheet
Transfer your answers to the following chart to discover your leadership wiring. Circle the letter corresponding to the answers you marked for each question. Then total your score at the bottom of each column.

Question	Doer	Thinker	Relater	Mover
1	A	B	C	D
2	C	D	A	B
3	B	A	D	C
4	D	C	B	A
5	A	B	D	C
6	B	D	C	A
7	C	A	B	D
8	A	C	D	B
9	B	D	A	C
10	D	B	C	A
Total				

Your highest total score is your primary leadership type. Write the name of your leadership type in the space below. If another type scored a close second, write the name of that type as your supporting type. If no other type scored close, then leave that space blank.

My primary leadership type: _____

My supporting leadership type (if any): _____

What Do the Leadership Types Mean?

The four ways leaders are wired are Doer, Thinker, Relater, and Mover. Each one shows a primary concern about an ingredient for a good team: getting something done, developing solutions, getting along, and accomplishing the goal.

Doers are primarily concerned about the tasks to be accomplished by the team. They like to focus on the task at hand, make checklists, get things organized, correct errors, and hit deadlines. Doers want the team to get it right.

Thinkers are primarily concerned about generating new ideas and solving team problems. They like to gather information, analyze a situation, brainstorm new ideas, develop plans, be creative, and get all the pieces working together. Thinkers want the team to develop creative solutions.

Relaters are primarily concerned about people and team relationships. They like to get to know the other team members, build relationships, encourage others, be a good listener, and be supportive. Relaters want the team members to get along.

Movers are primarily concerned about achieving goals and getting the team from here to there. Movers like to accept challenges, set goals, get others involved, make decisions, take appropriate risks, and persevere over difficulties. Movers want the team to win.

Every team needs to get along, to get something done, to develop solutions, and to accomplish the goal. Each leadership type addresses one of these four important ingredients. Next, you will compare all four types to confirm your score and find ways to improve the way you lead a team.

Leadership Type Grid

On the next page is a comparison of the four leadership types. Read through all of the descriptions to discover how people behave like you or unlike you as they lead or contribute to a team. Using a highlighter or pen, mark all of the tendencies that describe you. Then focus on your primary type and mark one or two steps you can take to become a more effective team member or team leader.

Doer		Thinker	
Concerned primarily about tasks to be accomplished by the team		Concerned primarily about generating new ideas and solving team problems	
Tendencies in a team setting may include:	*To be more effective as a team leader:*	*Tendencies in a team setting may include:*	*To be more effective as a team leader:*
• Focusing on the task at hand • Organizing the work of others • Making checklists • Starting and completing projects • Improving the process • Setting and meeting deadlines • Correcting errors • Wanting to get the work done • Wanting the team to get it right	• Be sensitive to needs of others • Avoid being over controlling • Share the workload • Show respect for team members • Show appreciation for efforts of others • Be willing to try new procedures • Avoid attitude of using people • Commit to building relationships	• Thinking ahead • Being creative • Gathering information • Analyzing a situation • Talking about issues in the group • Brainstorming new ideas • Developing plans • Getting pieces to work together • Wanting to solve team problems	• Avoid needing to be right all the time • Avoid bogging down in detail • Don't criticize other team members • Show respect for people • Don't be a loner • Be willing to take responsibility • Be more positive and optimistic • Commit to being a part of the team

Relater		Mover	
Concerned primarily about people and team relationships		Concerned primarily about goals and getting the team from here to there	
Tendencies in a team setting may include:	*To be more effective as a team leader:*	*Tendencies in a team setting may include:*	*To be more effective as a team leader:*
• Building relationships • Being supportive and loyal • Showing appreciation • Encouraging others • Acknowledging someone's effort • Being a good listener • Being agreeable • Sticking with the team • Wanting people to get along	• Be aware of what needs to be done • Pay attention to the schedule • Be willing to share your ideas • Be flexible and open to change • Ask for help in prioritizing work • Avoid withdrawing when people disagree • Commit to reaching team goals	• Setting goals • Accepting challenges • Taking charge • Wanting immediate results • Getting others involved • Making quick decisions • Taking appropriate risks • Persevering over difficulties • Wanting the team to win	• Be open to ideas of others • Get the facts and details • Avoid unnecessary risks • Be patient with team members • Avoid being demanding or bossy • Strive to remain humble • Respect authorities over you • Commit to sharing leadership

In what ways are you using your leadership wiring in God's kingdom? Are there any ways you are misusing or not using your leadership wiring?

Growth Steps
What is one step you can take this week to be more effective in your leadership?

Spiritual Gifts Assessment

After learning your wiring and how this fits within your leadership, it is vital to know exactly how Jesus has uniquely gifted you with special abilities to help in your Kingdom work. Just as God equipped Moses with specific gifts to help him lead the Israelites, God has also equipped you with spiritual gifts to help you live out his mission in your life.

Your awareness of your gifts and your ability within your gifts will grow over time as you mature spiritually, continually striving to spend time with God and grow in your relationship with him. As you use your gifts, your confidence in them will also grow.

This assessment was designed to help you identify your spiritual gifts. As with any assessment, your results will only be as accurate as the answers you give. Be sure to answer based on who you really are, not who you would like to be or who others think you ought to be.

Read the statements on the following pages carefully. Enter your ratings on the Response Sheet at the end of the assessment based on how well the statement describes you, using the following scale:

5	*Definitely Me*
4	*Very Much Like Me*
3	*Somewhat Like Me*
2	*Not Much Like Me*
1	*Definitely Not Me*

		Definitely me	Very much like me	Somewhat like me	Not much like me	Definitely not me
1.	I regularly encourage others to trust God, even when circumstances seem bleak.	5	4	3	2	1
2.	Others see me as caring and sensitive, and open up to me about their feelings.	5	4	3	2	1
3.	I willingly accept responsibility for leading groups that lack direction or motivation.	5	4	3	2	1
4.	I feel compelled to tell others about the inconsistencies I see and their impact.	5	4	3	2	1
5.	I seem better able than most people to sense when others are in need of a lift.	5	4	3	2	1
6.	I find it easy to engage non-believers in conversations about spiritual matters.	5	4	3	2	1
7.	I feel like a partner with the people and organizations I support financially.	5	4	3	2	1
8.	Others often ask me to research topics they want to understand more fully.	5	4	3	2	1
9.	I enjoy guiding and supporting individuals and groups seeking to learn and grow.	5	4	3	2	1
10.	Others see me as highly organized and look for my help in managing projects.	5	4	3	2	1
11.	I find that I am more adventurous and willing to take risks than most people.	5	4	3	2	1
12.	I enjoy analyzing difficult problems and discovering simple, practical solutions.	5	4	3	2	1
13.	I often seem to see matters of injustice or unfairness more clearly than other people.	5	4	3	2	1
14.	I enjoy working unrecognized behind the scenes to support the work of others.	5	4	3	2	1
15.	When I teach, I communicate clearly, and find it easy to engage people in learning.	5	4	3	2	1

		Definitely me	Very much like me	Somewhat like me	Not much like me	Definitely not me
16.	I am confident that God helps us to do great things when we trust him.	5	4	3	2	1
17.	I am easily moved by others' experience of heartache or suffering.	5	4	3	2	1
18.	I adjust my leadership style to work well with a variety of individuals or groups.	5	4	3	2	1
19.	I seem better able than most people to see the truth of what is really going on.	5	4	3	2	1
20.	Others see me as a positive, optimistic person who can make others feel good.	5	4	3	2	1
21.	I seem to be more concerned than most to share the Gospel with non-believers.	5	4	3	2	1
22.	I feel deep satisfaction knowing my giving is making a real difference.	5	4	3	2	1
23.	I enjoy becoming more of an expert on a topic, and sharing my knowledge with others.	5	4	3	2	1
24.	I am more willing than other people to invest time in helping others grow as believers.	5	4	3	2	1
25.	I enjoy being relied upon to organize people and tasks to meet a goal.	5	4	3	2	1
26.	Others see me as a change agent and look to me to lead new undertakings.	5	4	3	2	1
27.	I frequently am able to see potential solutions to problems that others cannot.	5	4	3	2	1
28.	Others see me as a person of strong convictions and willing to speak out.	5	4	3	2	1
29.	I find fulfillment in faithfully performing tasks others see as unglamorous.	5	4	3	2	1
30.	I am confident in my ability to help others learn and apply knowledge and skills.	5	4	3	2	1

		Definitely me	Very much like me	Somewhat like me	Not much like me	Definitely not me
31.	I think I am more confident than most in trusting God, even in the hard times.	5	4	3	2	1
32.	I enjoy helping people that others may regard as undeserving or beyond help.	5	4	3	2	1
33.	I can successfully motivate, guide, and manage others to reach important goals.	5	4	3	2	1
34.	Others see me as insightful, a good judge of people and situations.	5	4	3	2	1
35.	People often seek me out when they are looking for affirmation or encouragement.	5	4	3	2	1
36.	Others see me as being confident in my faith, and ready and willing to share it.	5	4	3	2	1
37.	I give more generously than most people to church and other worthwhile causes.	5	4	3	2	1
38.	I share what I know confidently and clearly, helping others to understand.	5	4	3	2	1
39.	Others see me as a patient, supportive person who brings out the best in others.	5	4	3	2	1
40.	I am skilled at planning, organizing, and managing even complex projects.	5	4	3	2	1
41.	I am always looking for new experiences and love bringing about change.	5	4	3	2	1
42.	When asked to help solve a problem, people usually end up taking my advice.	5	4	3	2	1
43.	I feel a strong sense of responsibility to take a stand for what is right and true.	5	4	3	2	1
44.	I can see how my support with the little things helps others accomplish more.	5	4	3	2	1
45.	I believe I am more motivated to want to help others learn than most people.	5	4	3	2	1

		Definitely me	Very much like me	Somewhat like me	Not much like me	Definitely not me
46.	Others see me as having strong faith, able to provide spiritual encouragement.	5	4	3	2	1
47.	It makes me happy to bring comfort, hope, and joy to people facing difficulties.	5	4	3	2	1
48.	I seem better able than most to help a group work together to achieve its goals.	5	4	3	2	1
49.	I always look below the surface to try to see the truth about people and situations.	5	4	3	2	1
50.	I am drawn to people who are confused or troubled, and try to cheer them up.	5	4	3	2	1
51.	In my relationships with non-believers, I regularly find ways to share my faith.	5	4	3	2	1
52.	It is important to manage my finances well so I can support causes I believe in.	5	4	3	2	1
53.	I like sharing knowledge that improves others' understanding and effectiveness.	5	4	3	2	1
54.	I willingly help others to grow in their faith and to improve their Christian walk.	5	4	3	2	1
55.	I enjoy helping a group to work efficiently and effectively to complete a project.	5	4	3	2	1
56.	I enjoy the challenge of trying new things, despite the unknowns or risks involved.	5	4	3	2	1
57.	I seem to see practical solutions to problems more readily than others.	5	4	3	2	1
58.	I am willing to speak out on matters of right and wrong even if unpopular.	5	4	3	2	1
59.	I seem more willing than most to pitch in wherever I can without being asked.	5	4	3	2	1
60.	Others see me as someone who can make difficult concepts easier to learn.	5	4	3	2	1

		Definitely me	Very much like me	Somewhat like me	Not much like me	Definitely not me
61.	I find it natural and easy to trust God to answer prayer for myself and others.	5	4	3	2	1
62.	I seem more compassionate than most, especially with people who are hurting.	5	4	3	2	1
63.	Others naturally look to me to lead, especially when facing big challenges.	5	4	3	2	1
64.	I can see through phoniness, deception, or error, usually before others are able to.	5	4	3	2	1
65.	I challenge people to look for and affirm the good in themselves and others.	5	4	3	2	1
66.	I like people to know I am a Christian and want them to ask me about my faith.	5	4	3	2	1
67.	I willingly contribute to projects needing my support or people in financial need.	5	4	3	2	1
68.	I think I am better than most people at gathering and sharing information.	5	4	3	2	1
69.	I see the things that hold people back and find ways to help them overcome.	5	4	3	2	1
70.	I think I am more organized than most, better able to manage complex tasks.	5	4	3	2	1
71.	My ability to adapt to new situations makes me comfortable with change.	5	4	3	2	1
72.	Others see me as having a lot of common sense and ask me for advice.	5	4	3	2	1
73.	I am comfortable challenging others to change their thoughts and actions.	5	4	3	2	1
74.	Others see me as always willing to pitch in and do even the smallest routine tasks.	5	4	3	2	1
75.	I enjoy preparing to teach—organizing and planning interesting learning experiences.	5	4	3	2	1

Scoring Guide

Response Sheet

Enter your responses in the appropriate boxes below. Place your score for question #1 in the box marked #1, and so on. After transferring all of your scores, add up the scores for each row and place the total in the column on the right.

					Totals
1. 3	16. 4	31. 4	46. 3	61. 3	1. 17
2. 4	17. 4	32. 4	47. 3	62. 3	2. 18
3. 4	18. 3	33. 3	48. 3	63. 3	3. 16
4. 4	19. 4	34. 3	49. 3	64. 3	4. 17
5. 4	20. 3	35. 3	50. 3	65. 3	5. 16
6. 3	21. 3	36. 3	51. 3	66. 3	6. 15
7. 2	22. 4	37. 4	52. 3	67. 3	7. 16
8. 2	23. 4	38. 4	53. 3	68. 3	8. 18
9. 4	24. 4	39. 4	54. 3	69. 3	9. 18
10. 4	25. 3	40. 3	55. 3	70. 3	10.
11. 5	26. 3	41. 3	56. 3	71. 3	11.
12. 2	27. 3	42. 3	57. 3	72. 3	12.
13. 4	28. 4	43. 3	58. 3	73. 3	13.
14. 3	29. 4	44. 4	59. 3	74. 3	14.
15. 3	30. 3	45. 3	60. 3	75. 3	15.

Enter your totals from the *Response Sheet* in the appropriate spaces below.

	Gift	**Description**
1.	**Believing** *(Faith)*	Believing is a special, God-given ability to trust God's will and act on it with an unwavering belief in God's concern, presence, and active participation.
2.	**Comforting** *(Mercy)*	Comforting is a special, God-given ability to understand and come alongside people who are troubled or suffering, bringing them comfort, insight, and hope.
3.	**Directing** *(Leadership)*	Directing is a special, God-given ability to instill vision, motivate, and guide people to work together effectively to achieve worthwhile goals.
4.	**Discerning** *(Discernment)*	Discerning is a special, God-given ability to distinguish between truth and error, good and evil, and to show good judgment in matters involving character and relationships.
5.	**Encouraging** *(Exhortation)*	Encouraging is a special, God-given ability to affirm, uplift, and restore confidence to individuals who are feeling discouraged or defeated.
6.	**Evangelizing** *(Evangelism)*	Evangelizing is a special, God-given ability to effectively communicate the Good News of Jesus Christ to non-believers so they can respond and begin to grow in their faith.
7.	**Giving** *(Contributing)*	Giving is a special, God-given ability to contribute cheerfully, generously, and regularly to the church and other important ministries, causes, and people in need.
8.	**Learning** *(Knowledge)*	Learning is a special, God-given ability to gather, analyze, and share information appropriately with others, leading to greater understanding and insight.
9.	**Mentoring** *(Pastor/Shepherding)*	Mentoring is a special, God-given ability to guide and support individuals or groups as they grow in their faith and in their capacity for ministry.
10.	**Organizing** *(Administration)*	Organizing is a special, God-given ability to plan, organize tasks, and follow through so that complex projects are completed efficiently and effectively.
11.	**Pioneering** *(Apostleship)*	Pioneering is a special, God-given ability to launch new ventures or lead change, confidently moving forward despite uncertainty or risk.
12.	**Problem Solving** *(Wisdom)*	Problem Solving is a special, God-given ability to provide practical advice that leads to timely, effective resolution of problems.
13.	**Speaking Out** *(Prophet)*	Speaking Out is a special, God-given ability to declare God's truth boldly and publicly for the purpose of correction or instruction.
14.	**Supporting** *(Helps)*	Supporting is a special, God-given ability to provide practical, behind-the-scenes help that frees others to accomplish more than they might otherwise be capable of achieving.
15.	**Teaching** *(Teacher)*	Teaching is a special, God-given ability to organize and clearly communicate knowledge and skills to others, and to motivate them to master and apply what they are learning.

Review your scores from the previous page. Identify the 2 or 3 spiritual gifts that appear to be your strongest (higher score being stronger) and list these below.

My spiritual gifts may include:

_____

_____

_____

Next, take some time to learn more about these gifts. For each of your strongest gifts, review the gift summaries on the following pages. Take time to understand what each gift is and the unique contribution it enables you to make when you use it wisely. Think of examples where you have been able to use each gift effectively. How did it feel? What results did you achieve? Have you ever experienced any of the problems described in the Potential Pitfalls section of the summary?

Believing

(Faith)

Basic Definition
Believing is a special, God-given ability to trust God's will and act on it, with an unwavering belief in God's concern, presence, and active participation.

Unique Leadership Contribution
People with this gift trust God to answer prayer and encourage others to do so, confident in God's help, even in difficult times or in the face of opposition.

This Gift in Scripture
This gift is listed in 1 Corinthians 12:9 where it is usually translated as "faith" or "special faith."

This Gift in Use
People with this gift keep moving forward with confidence, undaunted by obstacles, encouraged by a deeply-rooted belief in God's unending faithfulness and constant care. They are also often the true prayer warriors of the church, lifting its needs to the Lord and seeking his will. When this gift is absent in the church, people can come to doubt God's goodness or his love and concern for his people.

This Gift in a Team
When the going gets tough, people with this gift step up and encourage the rest of the team to keep moving forward, trusting God for strength, guidance, and success.

Typical Strengths
People with this gift tend to be confident, optimistic, prayerful, and reliant on God. By declaring their own trust in God, they encourage others to move forward in faith too.

Potential Pitfalls
People with this gift can become weary and discouraged—or even angry and critical—when others do not share their confidence in God's concern or participation. Using this gift wisely involves remembering and reminding others of the many examples of God's faithfulness in the past, even during the bleakest times.

Comforting

(Mercy)

Basic Definition
Comforting is a special, God-given ability to understand and come alongside people who are troubled or suffering, bringing them comfort, insight, and hope.

Unique Leadership Contribution
People with this gift patiently and compassionately help hurting people deal with painful experiences, even those whom others feel are undeserving or beyond help.

This Gift in Scripture
This gift is listed in Romans 12:8 where it is usually translated as "showing mercy" or "showing kindness."

This Gift in Use
People with this gift have a unique capacity for providing timely, practical support to hurting people, seemingly with endless patience, compassion, and joy in their hearts. They respond caringly to others' deepest needs, yet are able to look past their problems and circumstances and see their true worth as if through the eyes of God. When this gift is absent in the church, those who are truly needy will receive too little attention.

This Gift in a Team
In the life of any team, there will be times when people need, more than anything, to be comforted by someone who comes alongside even as others pull back.

Typical Strengths
People with this gift tend to be caring, sensitive, and tolerant—natural burden bearers. They sense when people are down, and find ways to be there for them.

Potential Pitfalls
Sometimes, people with this gift become weighed down from carrying the burdens of others. Another problem may be that they may unintentionally enable others to avoid facing their difficulties or making hard choices. Using this gift wisely involves helping hurting people deal with the underlying causes of their problems, and not covering them up.

Directing

(Leadership)

Basic Definition
Directing is a special, God-given ability to instill vision, motivate, and guide people to work together effectively to achieve worthwhile goals.

Unique Leadership Contribution
People with this gift willingly take responsibility for directing groups, managing people, and resources effectively, and challenging others to perform at the highest level.

This Gift in Scripture
This gift is listed in Romans 12:8 where it is usually translated as "leadership" or "he who leads."

This Gift in Use
People with this gift help others aspire to and achieve lofty goals. They understand the importance of getting people to perform at their best, both individually and as a group. They relish the opportunity to be in a position of leadership where they can influence the performance of a group that is doing meaningful work. When this gift is absent in the church, people will find themselves falling well short of their potential.

This Gift in a Team
People with this gift are the natural leaders that all teams need to ensure that their efforts are guided by a vision worth pursuing and strategies worth implementing.

Typical Strengths
People with this gift tend to be goal-oriented, decisive, inspiring, and persuasive. They will tend to rise to the top in most groups, emerging naturally as the leader.

Potential Pitfalls
People with this gift need to avoid being over-confident in their own abilities and possibly pushing others away by their perceived arrogance or forcefulness. They can also get stuck in their own ways of doing things, becoming intolerant of others. Using this gift wisely involves building credibility, mutual trust, and support with followers.

Discerning

(Discernment)

Basic Definition
Discerning is a special, God-given ability to distinguish between truth and error, good and evil, and to show good judgment in matters involving character and relationships.

Unique Leadership Contribution
People with this gift reliably distinguish between truth and error, good and evil, readily seeing through phoniness and deceit to perceive what is really going on.

This Gift in Scripture
This gift is listed in 1 Corinthians 12:10 where it is usually translated as "distinguishing between spirits" or "discerning of spirits."

This Gift in Use
People with this gift are unusually capable of recognizing inconsistencies in relationships, behavior, motives, teaching, and everyday practices. They quickly perceive the truth about these things, understand the potential consequences, and warn others to be on guard in order to avoid potentially risky situations. When this gift is absent in the church, people fall prey to false teaching or misguided leadership.

This Gift in a Team
At times, a team will find itself in situations where things are not really as they appear and must rely on the finely-tuned perception of someone with this gift to see the truth.

Typical Strengths
People with this gift are insightful, intuitive, and objective. They will often see things differently than others and will strongly defend their views if challenged.

Potential Pitfalls
People with this gift may need to work hard to avoid being seen by others as harsh and inflexible when sharing their insights, especially when their perceptions run counter to what others are thinking. Using this gift wisely involves taking the time to hear others' opinions, and to seek and share evidence that confirms what they think they are seeing.

Encouraging

(Exhortation)

Basic Definition
Encouraging is a special, God-given ability to affirm, uplift, and restore confidence to individuals who are feeling discouraged or defeated.

Unique Leadership Contribution
People with this gift sense the needs of others, particularly when they are feeling down, and provide much-appreciated reassurance and cheering up so they can carry on.

This Gift in Scripture
This gift is listed in Romans 12:8 where it is usually translated as "encouraging" or "exhortation."

This Gift in Use
People with this gift readily tune in to others who are in need of a boost. Typically positive and enthusiastic, they sense how others feel and what they need to do to encourage them. Sometimes they challenge or confront, and at other times they cheer up, applaud, or affirm. Whatever the situation, their goal is to help others feel better about themselves. When this gift is absent from a church, people can feel overwhelmed and give up.

This Gift in a Team
Every team needs at least one, dedicated cheerleader, and that's a role people with this gift relish. When the going gets tough, they help people stay up and keep moving toward the goal.

Typical Strengths
People with this gift are usually sensitive, positive, and enthusiastic. They see the good in every person, the possibilities in every problem, and the light at the end of the tunnel.

Potential Pitfalls
At times, people with this gift can come across as too simplistic or idealistic. Others don't always appreciate their sunny disposition and unwavering optimism. Using this gift wisely involves acknowledging the reality of the circumstances people are facing and finding ways to offer not only encouragement, but also concrete, practical help.

Evangelizing

(Evangelism)

Basic Definition
Evangelizing is a special, God-given ability to effectively communicate the Good News of Jesus Christ to non-believers so they can respond and begin to grow in their faith.

Unique Leadership Contribution
People with this gift find opportunities to build relationships with non-believers, comfortably share their faith, and invite people to decide to follow Christ.

This Gift in Scripture
This gift is listed in Ephesians 4:11 where it is usually translated as "evangelists."

This Gift in Use
People with this gift communicate the Gospel with ease and effectiveness. They seek opportunities to build relationships with non-believers in order to demonstrate the Good News of God's love in practical ways, and to get to know people better. This allows them to share their faith in ways that speak directly to the deepest needs of others. When this gift is absent from a church, people are reluctant to witness and outreach to non-believers will be ineffective.

This Gift in a Team
No matter what the primary focus of a team, there will be many opportunities to share the Gospel, and someone with this gift is most likely to recognize these opportunities and respond.

Typical Strengths
People with this gift tend to be social, secure in their faith, open, and candid. They willingly share their faith, doing so naturally and without much fear of rejection or ridicule.

Potential Pitfalls
At times, people with this gift will become discouraged when they are not seeing a response to their evangelistic efforts. Over time, they may become mechanical in their approach, or too aggressive, and turn off non-believers. Using this gift wisely means talking about your relationship with God, and inviting others to begin one of their own.

Giving

(Contributing)

Basic Definition
Giving is a special, God-given ability to contribute cheerfully, generously, and regularly to the church and other important ministries, causes, and people in need.

Unique Leadership Contribution
People with this gift manage their personal resources well, contributing as much as possible to people and organizations working to meet needs that are important to them.

This Gift in Scripture
This gift is listed in Romans 12:8 where it is usually translated as "contributing to the needs of others" or "he who gives."

This Gift in Use
People with this gift look for ways to increase their giving to the ministries, causes, and needy individuals they are most committed to supporting. They willingly limit spending on themselves and commit themselves to regular giving. They tend to see themselves as partners with those whose work they support and follow their work closely. When this gift is missing from the church, ministries will lack the resources required to fulfill their mission.

This Gift in a Team
People who are generous givers are often the best individuals to challenge others to do the same, making them a very effective agent for acquiring the resources the team needs.

Typical Strengths
People with this gift tend to be generous, conscientious, prudent, and resourceful. They look beyond their own needs, and see the benefit of meeting the needs of others.

Potential Pitfalls
Sometimes, people with this gift may be tempted to use their resources to pursue a pet project of their own. Or, they can feel unappreciated if their generosity is not adequately recognized. Using this gift wisely involves acknowledging that all we have comes from God and being grateful for the resources we have that we can use for his glory.

Learning

(Knowledge)

Basic Definition
Learning is a special, God-given ability to gather, analyze, and share information appropriately with others, leading to greater understanding and insight.

Unique Leadership Contribution
People with this gift research topics of interest to themselves or others, organize their findings systematically, and share what they have learned with others.

This Gift in Scripture
This gift is listed in 1 Corinthians 12:8 where it is usually translated "message of knowledge," "word of knowledge," or "gift of special knowledge."

This Gift in Use
People with this gift are born researchers who love to accumulate and share information. Their unique interest leads them to keep exploring a subject to gain a deeper understanding and more useful information. They enjoy being invited to share their knowledge, helping others quickly gain deeper insight into important matters. When this gift is missing from the church, decisions and plans will be based on inadequate understanding and will eventually fail.

This Gift in a Team
Often people with this gift become a "walking library" of useful information on a wide range of topics crucial to the team's work, as well as the keeper of its learning history.

Typical Strengths
People with this gift tend to be inquisitive, analytical, and proud of their accumulated expertise, with a large appetite for acquiring and sharing information.

Potential Pitfalls
People with this gift need to remember that their latest discovery may not be as exciting to others as to them. They can also fall into the trap of being proud of what they know, even feeling superior to others as a result. The wise use of this gift involves learning to respond to others' self-identified needs for greater understanding in a given area.

Mentoring

(Pastor/Shepherding)

Basic Definition
Mentoring is a special, God-given ability to guide and support individuals or groups as they grow in their faith and in their capacity for ministry.

Unique Leadership Contribution
People with this gift are committed to bringing out the best in others, patiently but firmly nurturing them in their development as whole persons, often on a long-term basis.

This Gift in Scripture
This gift is listed in Ephesians 4:11 where it is usually translated as "pastors."

This Gift in Use
People with this gift willingly accept responsibility for guiding and protecting people who they believe God has entrusted to their care. They identify others' strengths and limitations, and look for timely opportunities to challenge them to grow. Their long-term concern for people makes them highly trusted advisors and coaches. When this gift is missing from the church, people will remain weak in their faith and their Christian walk.

This Gift in a Team
Often people with this gift support a team by supporting its members in an ongoing process of personal and ministry development, both as individuals and as a group.

Typical Strengths
People with this gift tend to be nurturing, growth-minded, and discipleship-oriented. They will look for ways to maximize each person's growth and contribution.

Potential Pitfalls
People with this gift need to be careful about viewing certain people as projects. They may also have difficulty saying no, which can lead to burn-out. Using this gift wisely involves recognizing and maintaining appropriate boundaries, developing healthy relationships that avoid creating dependency between or among those involved.

Organizing

(Administration)

Basic Definition
Organizing is a special, God-given ability to plan, organize tasks, and follow through so that complex projects are completed efficiently and effectively.

Unique Leadership Contribution
People with this gift ensure the success of a project by clarifying goals, developing detailed plans, delegating tasks, monitoring performance, and managing follow-through.

This Gift in Scripture
This gift is listed in 1 Corinthians 12:28 where it is usually translated as "administration," "governments," or "those who can get others to work together."

This Gift in Use
People with this gift have the capacity to coordinate people, tasks, and resources even in very complex circumstances. Working within the context of the project's goals, they focus on both doing the right things and doing things right. They know how to bring order out of chaos in organizations, always able to see how everything fits together. When this gift is missing from the church, people will become frustrated by confusion, waste, and the inability to get things done.

This Gift in a Team
With so many tasks and people to manage, complexity is a fact of life for most teams. People with this gift develop the systems, processes, and plans to make it all work.

Typical Strengths
People with this gift tend to be highly-organized, thorough, clear-thinking, and conscientious. They are comfortable with detail and strive for order and harmony.

Potential Pitfalls
People with this gift must be careful not to frustrate other leaders who don't share their enthusiasm for thoroughness and detail. Also, when things aren't going well, they can sometimes seem to be "using people" simply to accomplish tasks. Using this gift wisely involves balancing task requirements and deadlines with people's needs and feelings.

Pioneering

(Apostleship)

Basic Definition
Pioneering is a special, God-given ability to launch new ventures or lead change, confidently moving forward despite uncertainty or risk.

Unique Leadership Contribution
People with this gift lead the way in spearheading change, testing out new ideas, or leading innovation, often producing breakthroughs in growth or effectiveness.

This Gift in Scripture
This gift is listed in 1 Corinthians 12:28 and Ephesians 4:11 where it is usually translated as "apostles."

This Gift in Use
People with this gift have little fear of the unknown, and an appetite for adventure and even risk. They look for opportunities for growth and change, seeking to move beyond the status quo. Where others get anxious, they get excited. Where others see obstacles, they see opportunities. They always look forward to the next challenge. When this gift is missing from the church, people will find it very difficult to bring about change or start something new.

This Gift in a Team
Even high-performing teams can sometimes find themselves in a rut. It takes someone with this gift to stir things up, keep looking ahead, and push for much-needed changes.

Typical Strengths
People with this gift tend to be adventurous, risk-taking, adaptable, and confident. Being natural entrepreneurs, they have a make-it-happen approach to the future.

Potential Pitfalls
At times, people with this gift will move too quickly and get ahead of others. They may find themselves disconnected from the supporters they need, sometimes even alienating them. Using this gift wisely involves engaging others in creating a shared vision and in making plans to get there.

Problem Solving

(Wisdom)

Basic Definition
Problem Solving is a special, God-given ability to provide practical advice that leads to timely, effective resolution of problems.

Unique Leadership Contribution
People with this gift can often identify simple, practical solutions to problems, helping others find ways to get unstuck and confidently move toward their goals.

This Gift in Scripture
This gift is listed in 1 Corinthians 12:8 where it is usually translated as "message of wisdom," "word of wisdom," or "the ability to give wise advice."

This Gift in Use
People with this gift see solutions where others may only see roadblocks. They seem to be able to cut through confusion and conflict and see how to overcome obstacles. They are good at figuring out the best action to take in a given situation. Blessed with an uncommon amount of common sense, they offer practical advice that others willingly follow. When this gift is missing from the church, people may repeat past mistakes or continue doing things the hard way.

This Gift in a Team
Every team runs into problems and needs someone who can offer practical advice to get the team back on track as well as help the team avoid getting bogged down in the first place.

Typical Strengths
People with this gift will tend to be logical, sensible, observant, and highly practical. They will see options others miss and carefully choose the most effective way forward.

Potential Pitfalls
People with this gift may be tempted to hold back from sharing their insights until someone invites them to do so, perhaps because they have learned that others are not always open to advice. Using this gift wisely involves learning how to share important insights and suggestions in ways that others can understand and embrace them.

Speaking Out

(Prophet)

Basic Definition
Speaking Out is a special, God-given ability to declare God's truth boldly and publicly for the purpose of correction or instruction.

Unique Leadership Contribution
People with this gift challenge others to change their behavior by speaking out clearly and convincingly about right and wrong, even where it may be unpopular.

This Gift in Scripture
This gift is listed in Romans 12:6, 1 Corinthians 12:10, 28, and Ephesians 4:11 where it is usually translated as "prophesying," "prophets," or "ability to prophesy."

This Gift in Use
People with this gift are especially attuned both to God's principles and to what is really going on in the world. They look for the right time and place to share what they feel must be said to influence others. They tend to see issues that others fail to see and feel compelled to speak out. When this gift is missing from the church, people can lose touch with God's heart and his will.

This Gift in a Team
Often people with this gift support a team by serving as a kind of "moral compass," challenging others to live up to biblical standards of right and wrong.

Typical Strengths
People with this gift will tend to be individualistic, opinionated, outspoken, and determined. They will see situations and issues in very clear, black-and-white terms.

Potential Pitfalls
At times, people with this gift will be difficult to be around because of their strong need to speak out, which may be perceived as overly judgmental and critical of others. Using this gift wisely involves being compassionate toward others and having a genuine desire to motivate others to change rather than a need to simply point out where they are wrong.

Supporting

(Helps)

Basic Definition
Supporting is a special, God-given ability to provide practical, behind-the-scenes help that frees others to accomplish more than they might otherwise be capable of achieving.

Unique Leadership Contribution
People with this gift usually like to work behind the scenes, supporting the work of others, cheerfully finding and doing small things that need doing, often without being asked.

This Gift in Scripture
This gift is listed in Romans 12:7 and 1 Corinthians 12:28 where it is usually translated as "helps," "serving," "ministry," "forms of assistance," or "those able to help others."

This Gift in Use
People with this gift take pride in doing well the seemingly small tasks others sometimes consider mundane or routine. They appreciate how their faithful assistance with these tasks pays off by freeing others to focus their attention on "higher level" tasks and enables them to use their gifts more fully. When this gift is missing from the church, leaders can become bogged down by details or worn out from trying to do everything alone.

This Gift in a Team
No one gets to do the glamorous work all of the time, but those with this gift willingly take on the more routine tasks, making it possible for high-performing teams to excel.

Typical Strengths
People with this gift tend to be flexible, easy-going, dependable, and humble. They take pride in serving others faithfully without concern for recognition or honor.

Potential Pitfalls
People with this gift often find it difficult to say no, causing them to overcommit, which leads to a loss of balance in their lives. Some also come to depend on what they do for others for their self-worth. Using this gift wisely involves recognizing that God values people for who they are, not what they do, and by maintaining a healthy, balanced life.

Teaching

(Teacher)

Basic Definition
Teaching is a special, God-given ability to organize and clearly communicate knowledge and skills to others, and to motivate them to master and apply what they are learning.

Unique Leadership Contribution
People with this gift identify the knowledge and skills others need to learn, and use creative approaches to help them learn willingly and effectively.

This Gift in Scripture
This gift is listed in Romans 12:7, 1 Corinthians 12:28, and Ephesians 4:11 where it is usually translated as "teaching" or "teacher."

This Gift in Use
People with this gift focus on helping others develop their knowledge and skill, including their knowledge of Christian principles. They begin by understanding the learning needs of others, and then look for teachable moments to engage people in creative, enjoyable learning activities that lead to knowledge and skill improvement. When this gift is missing from the church, people will not grow in depth of faith or capacity for ministry.

This Gift in a Team
Often people with this gift have the best feel for the strengths and limitations of the team. They often can tell what others need to learn and how to help them learn it.

Typical Strengths
People with this gift will usually be skilled at organizing ideas, creative, and enthusiastic. They have a special knack for making difficult concepts easier to learn.

Potential Pitfalls
The most common shortcoming of people with this gift is their tendency to over-teach, presenting too much content and not enough opportunity for reflection, review, and experimenting with application. Using this gift wisely involves continually "checking in" with the learners and adjusting to their motivation, pace, and learning style.

How often are you exercising or using your spiritual gifts? Were there any that surprised you?

Growth Steps
How can you use your gifts in leadership?

Before You Move On

Take some time to enter your results of the Leadership Wiring Assessment and the Spiritual Gifts Assessment into your Leadership Profile on page 92 of this book. Make sure to share your results for both of these assessments with another person you trust so that they can keep you accountable for growing in your newly found knowledge of your Leadership Design. Remember, everything you learn about leadership is only valuable if you apply it in life.

SMALL GROUP STUDY TIME TABLE

Below is a table outlining the content of this session along with an approximate time-frame, which you can adapt to meet the needs of your group. Please take notice that several items should be prepared by students before coming to the small group so as to maximize time.

Session Outline	Description	Approximate Timeframe
Leadership Design	A look at how individuals are wired and gifted for their roles in leadership. Discuss with group.	*10 minutes*
Bible on Leadership Design	An in-depth look at the life of Moses and his leadership design with additional questions (see below).	*15 minutes*
Leadership Wiring Assessment	An assessment determining the leadership wiring of an individual. Discuss results with group.	*Completed Before Small Group/15 minutes*
Life Application	Questions diving into how the group is using their leadership wiring.	*15 minutes*
Spiritual Gift Assessment	An assessment determining the spiritual gifts of an individual. Discuss results with group.	*Completed Before Small Group/15 minutes*
Life Application	Questions diving into how the group is using their spiritual gifts.	*15 minutes*
Group Activity	Divide group into pairs to share specific action plans (see below).	*10 minutes*

Additional Questions for the Moses Case Study

1. Read Exodus 2:13–14 in context with the rest of Exodus. Why do you suppose the Hebrew slave responded this way to Moses? How did God use this response and the repercussions of Moses' actions to bring about his will?

2. Why did Moses fear his skills and strengths were not enough for him to lead God's people to freedom? Do you ever fear your skills are not enough? Does this ever prevent you from taking a risk?

3. Why does God give spiritual gifts rather than just wiring individuals with those skills originally?

4. How do you suppose Moses' receiving of gifts impacted his own faith life?

Group Activity

Divide the group into pairs and have them share their specific Growth Steps for how they will use their leadership design (wiring and gifts) in the next week. Use the following questions for making applications:

- What are you going to do?
- Where are you going to do it?
- When are you going to do it?

Have each pair record their partner's application and then commit to praying for their partner and asking them at least once over the next week if they have accomplished their application goal.

BALANCING ACT

EVERY RUNNER knows that only half the race is up to their physical performance. The other half is in their head. That's why you find every coach giving their runners a pep talk before a race. The mental part of a race can make it or break it just as much as any physical ability can. It's the same way in leadership. A leader needs more than leadership skills, they need great character as well. When our skills and our character get out of balance, bad leadership happens. It's not hard to point out a bad leader. Not only is history full of them, but our sports teams, classes, communities, and governments are tainted by bad leaders. Some leaders trample people; other leaders get nothing done. It's sad, but true. In fact, truly great leaders only emerge when their skills and their character are in balance.

Every Leadership Skill must be balanced by Leadership Character Traits.

In this chapter, we've included both the 5 Leadership Skills that provide a step-by-step guide to leading a team toward the completion of a project and the 5 Character Traits that provide the bedrock of the leader's character. Coincidentally, these skills and traits go hand-in-hand with each other. Each skill is refined and sharpened by a coordinating character trait.

Take some time now to examine the Five Skills and Five Character Traits of a Leader.

The Five Skills and Five Character Traits of a Leader

1. Skill: Determine the Scope and Goals of the Project

Leaders must be able to envision the future. Start by determining what the end result of the project is and then work backward from there, setting short term goals that will lead your team to complete the job with excellence.

Question: What does this project/mission look like at the end? What is the effect of it?

Trait: Vision

Leaders see the finish line before anyone else – they look into the future and see what no one else can see. A leader, guided by prayer, dreams about the biggest accomplishments God will do through their team. This trait allows the leader to determine the scope for the project and the steps needed to reach it.

Action: Consistently (every day!) sit before God and ask what his vision is for the team and mission.

2. Skill: Calculate the People and Resources Needed to Complete the Project

Leaders must put the right people in the right positions in order for a team to perform at maximum potential. Leaders must also provide the resources to complete projects, whether that includes money, materials, or other necessities. The leader of the team must take time to think through what is exactly needed to achieve success.

Question: What resources and people do we need to complete this mission?

Trait: Wisdom

Wisdom is the knowledge of what is true or right coupled with just action. A leader must display quality discernment when faced with tough decisions. A leader needs wisdom to find the perfect balance between hard materials and caring for followers.

Action: In James 1:5, God promises us wisdom if we ask for it…each day, ask God for wisdom.

3. Skill: Cast the Vision

A clearly communicated vision can change everything. If leaders are able to articulate the vision powerfully (meaning passionately!), no obstacle will stand in the way of their mission. The leader must clearly communicate the "why" to all followers.

Question: Put yourself in your teammates' shoes. Does everyone know the "why" behind reaching the finish line, and does everyone know you're passionate about it?

Trait: Enthusiasm

For a leader to cast the vision to followers he or she must have optimism, creativity and a positive outlook. These things flow from a rock-solid "can-do" attitude. Enthusiasm creates a momentum for change that galvanizes followers around a common mission.

Action: Take the temperature of your followers' attitude. Are they unmotivated or are they embracing the mission? Cast the vision one more time this week, coupling it with enthusiasm.

4. Skill: Navigate the Obstacles

Navigating obstacles requires looking ahead and discovering what potential obstacles lie in the way, and then producing a plan for overcoming those obstacles before they sabotage the project. Leaders also need to establish healthy environments and deal with conflicts between personalities.

Question: What obstacles could prevent you from reaching the goals you set in the first skill of a leader?

Trait: Perseverance

Perseverance is a steady persistence in spite of difficulties, obstacles, or discouragement. Sometimes when we face obstacles, even ones we planned for, we want to reduce our initial goals to make them easier. A leader must fight this pressure with perseverance in order to insure completion.

Action: Write down what this project/mission could cost you (time, focus, energy, resources, relationships, opportunities, etc.). Now ask yourself, if it costs you all of these things, what is your commitment level?

5. Skill: Evaluate the Performance

Leaders need to ask, "How can we do this better?" Consistent, honest evaluation is the leader's tool to bring about growth in followers and to ensure excellence in all that his or her team does. Whether it is taking place in the middle of the project or the end, a leader must evaluate both the progress and the performance of everyone involved, offering feedback that is helpful along the way, while also celebrating accomplishments achieved by the team.

Question: In what ways can you and your followers improve? Now make an action plan to solve that problem. In what ways are you and your followers doing well? Now celebrate!

Trait: Honesty

When a leader displays honesty, they are truthful and sincere, even in moments where it does not benefit the leader. Honest leaders are free from deceit or fraud. Honesty takes courage and commitment. When leaders are honest with themselves and their followers, growth will happen. True evaluation never happens outside of honesty.

Action: Honesty starts with you. Before offering honest feedback to your followers about their performance, be honest with yourself. How do you need to grow as a leader? What will you do to grow in that area?

These five skills and traits are needed for every leader if they are going to successfully lead a team to greatness. Let's take some time and examine these leadership truths from a Biblical perspective.

The Bible on the Balancing Act

At the start of Nehemiah's book, he finds himself in a seemingly hopeless situation. Having grown up in captivity, Nehemiah knows all too well the stories of Jerusalem's destruction of the city walls, temple, and city itself. In the years that followed the destruction and enslavement, several different successful attempts were made to go back and rebuild the city walls and the temple. But during a visit from his brother, who had just returned from Jerusalem, Nehemiah learns that the walls that had been rebuilt had recently been destroyed again; the city was unprotected, at the whim of murderers and thieves.

Nehemiah is broken. He mourns for the brokenness of the city, and spends months in prayer. During this time, Nehemiah realizes he has been called to lead the restoration of Jerusalem and the people of Israel. From the start of his quest to the end, he put into action all five skills and character traits of a leader.

Read Nehemiah's story on the following pages. The same questions and actions for each skill and trait are scattered inside of his story, so as you read, do these two things:

1. Every time you see a highlighted character trait, pay attention to how Nehemiah lived out that leadership character trait.

2. Answer the questions that correspond to the leadership skills Nehemiah displayed.

Nehemiah's Story

VISION

They said to me, "Those who survived the exile and are back in the province are in great trouble and disgrace. The wall of Jerusalem is broken down, and its gates have been burned with fire."

When I heard these things, I sat down and wept. For some days I mourned and fasted and prayed before the God of heaven....

In the month of Nisan in the twentieth year of King Artaxerxes, when wine was brought for him, I took the wine and gave it to the king. I had not been sad in his presence before, so the king asked me, "Why does your face look so sad when you are not ill? This can be nothing but sadness of heart."

I was very much afraid, but I said to the king, "May the king live forever! Why should my face not look sad when the city where my ancestors are buried lies in ruins, and its gates have been destroyed by fire?"

The king said to me, "What is it you want?"

Then I prayed to the God of heaven, and I answered the king, "If it pleases the king and if your servant has found favor in his sight, let him send me to the city in Judah where my ancestors are buried so that I can rebuild it." —Nehemiah 1:3–4, 2:1–5

Leadership Skill Question *(Determine the Scope and Goals of the Project)*
What does this project/mission for Nehemiah look like at the end? What is the effect of
it?

_____

_____

_____

_____

*Then the king, with the queen sitting beside him, asked me, "How long will your
journey take, and when will you get back?" It pleased the king to send me; so I
set a time.*

WISDOM

*I also said to him, "If it pleases the king, may I have letters to the governors of
Trans-Euphrates, so that they will provide me safe-conduct until I arrive in Judah?
And may I have a letter to Asaph, keeper of the royal park, so he will give me
timber to make beams for the gates of the citadel by the temple and for the city
wall and for the residence I will occupy?" And because the gracious hand of my
God was on me, the king granted my requests. So I went to the governors of
Trans-Euphrates and gave them the king's letters. The king had also sent army
officers and cavalry with me.*
—Nehemiah 2:6–9

Leadership Skill Question *(Calculate the People and Resources Needed to Complete the Project)*
What resources and people did Nehemiah need to complete this mission?

_____

_____

_____

_____

Once Nehemiah got to Jerusalem and scouted out the ruined walls, he cast the vision for
the people.

*Then I said to them, "You see the trouble we are in: Jerusalem lies in ruins, and its
gates have been burned with fire. Come, let us rebuild the wall of Jerusalem, and
we will no longer be in disgrace." I also told them about the gracious hand of my
God upon me and what the king had said to me.*

They replied, "Let us start rebuilding." So they began this good work.
—Nehemiah 2:17–18

And again when the workers were tired and facing enemy threats, look what Nehemiah does…

After I looked things over, I stood up and said to the nobles, the officials and the rest of the people, "Don't be afraid of them. Remember the Lord, who is great and awesome, and fight for your families, your sons and your daughters, your wives and your homes."
—Nehemiah 4:14

Leadership Skill Question *(Cast the Vision)*
How does Nehemiah communicate the "why" behind reaching the finish line? How does he communicate his own passion about it?

_____

_____

_____

_____

When our enemies heard that we were aware of their plot and that God had frustrated it, we all returned to the wall, each to our own work. From that day on, half of my men did the work, while the other half were equipped with spears, shields, bows and armor. The officers posted themselves behind all the people of Judah who were building the wall. Those who carried materials did their work with one hand and held a weapon in the other, and each of the builders wore his sword at his side as he worked. But the man who sounded the trumpet stayed with me.

Then I said to the nobles, the officials and the rest of the people, "The work is extensive and spread out, and we are widely separated from each other along the wall. Wherever you hear the sound of the trumpet, join us there. Our God will fight for us!"…Neither I nor my brothers nor my men nor the guards with me took off our clothes; each had his weapon, even when he went for water.
—Nehemiah 4:15–20, 23

Leadership Skill Question *(Navigate the Obstacles)*
What obstacles could have prevented Nehemiah from reaching the goals he set?

_____

_____

_____

_____

At the dedication of the wall of Jerusalem, the Levites were sought out from where they lived and were brought to Jerusalem to celebrate joyfully the dedica-

tion with songs of thanksgiving and with the music of cymbals, harps and lyres.
The musicians also were brought together from the region around Jerusalem…I
had the leaders of Judah go up on top of the wall. I also assigned two large
choirs to give thanks.
—*Nehemiah12:27, 28a, 31a*

After Nehemiah had finished the walls and appointed leaders, he went back to King
Artexerxes. He stayed in Persia for some time, then he once again requested permission
from the king to go back to Jerusalem and check on things.

I also learned that the portions assigned to the Levites had not been given to
them, and that all the Levites and musicians responsible for the service had gone
back to their own fields. So I rebuked the officials and asked them, "Why is the
house of God neglected?" Then I called them together and stationed them at
their posts.

All Judah brought the tithes of grain, new wine and oil into the storerooms. I put
Shelemiah the priest, Zadok the scribe, and a Levite named Pedaiah in charge
of the storerooms and made Hanan son of Zaccur, the son of Mattaniah, their
assistant, because these men were considered trustworthy. They were made
responsible for distributing the supplies to their fellow Levites.
—*Nehemiah13:10–13*

Leadership Skill Question *(Evaluate the Performance)*
How did Nehemiah celebrate what the Israelites had done well? In what ways did they
need to improve? What was Nehemiah's action plan for improvement?

_____

_____

_____

_____

Your Balancing Act

Leadership Skills Test

Now that you have taken some time to look at a Biblical example of the 5 Skills and 5 Traits of a Leader, let's apply these truths to your own life. Below you will read a scenario that you very well could be put into as a student leader. Read the scenario and use the 5 Skills of a Leader to plan out this project.

Congratulations! You have been chosen to head up this month's Youth Service Day for the youth group. You are the student leader and everything dealing with planning and facilitating the service day falls into your hands. Each month your youth group selects a theme for the day and spends about 4 hours volunteering in that area. For example, past days have centered around babysitting, yard work, homeless outreach, food pantries, and city cleanup. On average, about 15 kids have shown up for each service day, but your youth pastor really wants to up that number this time. With over 100 students in the youth group, he feels like you can get more to help. You have about three weeks to plan and promote your service day. Below is a list of your responsibilities in planning the service day.

- Theme/Project
- Logistics (Where, When, How Long, How Much)
- Spiritual Focus
- Promotion and Advertising
- Team Care

Each of these areas requires special planning in order for the service day to be a success. Using what you learned from Nehemiah's example, put into practice the 5 Skills and 5 Traits as you go about planning the day. You must decide how to use them as you plan the day.

Determine the Scope and Goals of the Project

Question: What does this project/mission look like at the end? What is the effect of it?

_____

_____

_____

_____

_____

_____

_____

_____

Calculate the People and Resources Needed to Complete the Project

Question: What resources and people do we need to complete this mission?

_____

_____

_____

_____

_____

_____

_____

_____

_____

_____

_____

Cast the Vision

Question: Put yourself in your teammates' shoes. Does everyone know the "why" behind reaching the finish line, and does everyone know you're passionate about it?

_____

_____

_____

_____

_____

_____

_____

_____

_____

_____

_____

_____

Navigate the Obstacles

Question: What obstacles could prevent you from reaching the goals you set in the first skill of a leader?

_____

_____

_____

_____

_____

_____

_____

_____

_____

_____

_____

Evaluate the Performance

Question: In what ways can you and your followers improve? Now make an action plan to solve that problem. In what ways are you and your followers doing well? Now celebrate!

_____

_____

_____

_____

_____

_____

_____

_____

_____

_____

_____

_____

Since you can't fully evaluate the service day, take some time and evaluate your own work on planning this day. What leadership skill would you say is your strongest? What skill of a leader do you need the most work on?

Growth Steps
How can you improve both your strong skills and the areas you need improvement?

Leadership Character Traits Assessment

Character can be tough to determine. Churches discuss it frequently, so at this point most people know you must have good character, especially in leadership. But how do you know where your character lies? Sometimes it takes honest evaluation to discover certain truths about your leadership.

Below is an evaluation for you to take. It will help you in discovering how the 5 character traits of a leader exemplify themselves in your life.

You will fill out the first assessment, and then give the other 3 to key people in your life (parent, youth worker, peer) for their feedback on how you are doing. Be honest with yourself so that you can grow. This will be challenging, as honest evaluation is always difficult. But if you take this seriously and strive to improve in the areas suggested, your leadership will flourish. Good luck, and don't be afraid to be vulnerable.

Self Assessment
Rate yourself in each area on a scale from 1 to 10. Please take the time to also fill out the questions and Growth Steps areas.

Vision
Leaders see the finish line before anyone else—they look into the future and see what no one else can see. A leader, guided by prayer, dreams about the biggest accomplishments God will do through their team. This trait allows the leader to determine the scope for the project and the steps needed to reach it.

1	2	3	4	5	6	7	8	9	10
Needs Improvement									*Excellent*

Why did you give yourself that score? Growth Steps:

_____

_____

_____

Wisdom
Wisdom is the knowledge of what is true or right coupled with just action. A leader must display quality discernment when faced with tough decisions. A leader needs wisdom to find the perfect balance between hard materials and caring for followers.

1	2	3	4	5	6	7	8	9	10
Needs Improvement									*Excellent*

Why did you give yourself that score? Growth Steps:

_____

_____

_____

Enthusiasm

For a leader to cast the vision to followers he or she must have optimism, creativity, and a positive outlook. These things flow from a rock solid belief that life can be better. Enthusiasm creates a momentum for change that galvanizes followers for a common mission.

1	2	3	4	5	6	7	8	9	10
Needs Improvement									*Excellent*

Why did you give yourself that score? Growth Steps:

_____

_____

_____

Perseverance

Perseverance is a steady persistence in a course of action in spite of difficulties, obstacles, or discouragement. Sometimes when we face obstacles, even ones we planned for, we want to reduce our initial goals to make them easier. A leader must fight this pressure with perseverance in order to insure completion.

1	2	3	4	5	6	7	8	9	10
Needs Improvement									*Excellent*

Why did you give yourself that score? Growth Steps:

_____

_____

_____

Honesty

When a leader displays honesty, they are truthful and sincere, even in moments where it does not benefit the leader. Leaders who are honest are free from deceit or fraud. Honesty takes courage and commitment. When leaders are honest with themselves and their followers, growth will happen. True evaluation never happens outside of honesty.

1	2	3	4	5	6	7	8	9	10
Needs Improvement									*Excellent*

Why did you give yourself that score? Growth Steps:

_____

_____

_____

Parent Assessment

_____ is taking an assessment to grow in their Leadership Character Traits. Below are 5 traits that leaders must have. Please take the time to rate this person and offer comments and Growth Step Suggestions before returning it.

Vision

Leaders see the finish line before anyone else—they look into the future and see what no one else can see. A leader, guided by prayer, dreams about the biggest accomplishments God will do through their team. This trait allows the leader to determine the scope for the project and the steps needed to reach it.

| 1 | 2 | 3 | 4 | 5 | 6 | 7 | 8 | 9 | 10 |
| Needs Improvement | | | | | | | | | Excellent |

Comments and Growth Step Suggestions:

_____

_____

_____

Wisdom

Wisdom is the knowledge of what is true or right coupled with just action. A leader must display quality discernment when faced with tough decisions. A leader needs wisdom to find the perfect balance between hard materials and caring for followers.

| 1 | 2 | 3 | 4 | 5 | 6 | 7 | 8 | 9 | 10 |
| Needs Improvement | | | | | | | | | Excellent |

Comments and Growth Step Suggestions:

_____

_____

_____

Enthusiasm

For a leader to cast the vision to followers he or she must have optimism, creativity, and a positive outlook. These things flow from a rock solid belief that life can be better. Enthusiasm creates a momentum for change that galvanizes followers for a common mission.

| 1 | 2 | 3 | 4 | 5 | 6 | 7 | 8 | 9 | 10 |
| Needs Improvement | | | | | | | | | Excellent |

Comments and Growth Step Suggestions:

_____

_____

_____

Perseverance

Perseverance is a steady persistence in a course of action in spite of difficulties, obstacles, or discouragement. Sometimes when we face obstacles, even ones we planned for, we want to reduce our initial goals to make them easier. A leader must fight this pressure with perseverance in order to insure completion.

1	2	3	4	5	6	7	8	9	10
Needs Improvement									Excellent

Comments and Growth Step Suggestions:

_____

_____

_____

Honesty

When a leader displays honesty, they are truthful and sincere, even in moments where it does not benefit the leader. Leaders who are honest are free from deceit or fraud. Honesty takes courage and commitment. When leaders are honest with themselves and their followers, growth will happen. True evaluation never happens outside of honesty.

1	2	3	4	5	6	7	8	9	10
Needs Improvement									Excellent

Comments and Growth Step Suggestions:

_____

_____

_____

Youth Worker Assessment

_____ is taking an assessment to grow in their Leadership Character Traits. Below are 5 traits that leaders must have. Please take the time to rate this person and offer comments and Growth Step Suggestions before returning it.

Vision

Leaders see the finish line before anyone else—they look into the future and see what no one else can see. A leader, guided by prayer, dreams about the biggest accomplishments God will do through their team. This trait allows the leader to determine the scope for the project and the steps needed to reach it.

1	2	3	4	5	6	7	8	9	10
Needs Improvement									_Excellent_

Comments and Growth Step Suggestions:

_____

_____

_____

Wisdom

Wisdom is the knowledge of what is true or right coupled with just action. A leader must display quality discernment when faced with tough decisions. A leader needs wisdom to find the perfect balance between hard materials and caring for followers.

1	2	3	4	5	6	7	8	9	10
Needs Improvement									_Excellent_

Comments and Growth Step Suggestions:

_____

_____

_____

Enthusiasm

For a leader to cast the vision to followers he or she must have optimism, creativity, and a positive outlook. These things flow from a rock solid belief that life can be better. Enthusiasm creates a momentum for change that galvanizes followers for a common mission.

1	2	3	4	5	6	7	8	9	10
Needs Improvement									_Excellent_

Comments and Growth Step Suggestions:

_____

_____

_____

Perseverance

Perseverance is a steady persistence in a course of action in spite of difficulties, obstacles, or discouragement. Sometimes when we face obstacles, even ones we planned for, we want to reduce our initial goals to make them easier. A leader must fight this pressure with perseverance in order to insure completion.

1	2	3	4	5	6	7	8	9	10
Needs Improvement									*Excellent*

Comments and Growth Step Suggestions:

_____

_____

_____

Honesty

When a leader displays honesty, they are truthful and sincere, even in moments where it does not benefit the leader. Leaders who are honest are free from deceit or fraud. Honesty takes courage and commitment. When leaders are honest with themselves and their followers, growth will happen. True evaluation never happens outside of honesty.

1	2	3	4	5	6	7	8	9	10
Needs Improvement									*Excellent*

Comments and Growth Step Suggestions:

_____

_____

_____

Peer Assessment

_____ is taking an assessment to grow in their Leadership Character Traits. Below are 5 traits that leaders must have. Please take the time to rate this person and offer comments and Growth Step Suggestions before returning it.

Vision

Leaders see the finish line before anyone else—they look into the future and see what no one else can see. A leader, guided by prayer, dreams about the biggest accomplishments God will do through their team. This trait allows the leader to determine the scope for the project and the steps needed to reach it.

1	2	3	4	5	6	7	8	9	10
Needs Improvement									_Excellent_

Comments and Growth Step Suggestions:

_____

_____

_____

Wisdom

Wisdom is the knowledge of what is true or right coupled with just action. A leader must display quality discernment when faced with tough decisions. A leader needs wisdom to find the perfect balance between hard materials and caring for followers.

1	2	3	4	5	6	7	8	9	10
Needs Improvement									_Excellent_

Comments and Growth Step Suggestions:

_____

_____

_____

Enthusiasm

For a leader to cast the vision to followers he or she must have optimism, creativity, and a positive outlook. These things flow from a rock solid belief that life can be better. Enthusiasm creates a momentum for change that galvanizes followers for a common mission.

1	2	3	4	5	6	7	8	9	10
Needs Improvement									_Excellent_

Comments and Growth Step Suggestions:

_____

_____

_____

Perseverance

Perseverance is a steady persistence in a course of action in spite of difficulties, obstacles, or discouragement. Sometimes when we face obstacles, even ones we planned for, we want to reduce our initial goals to make them easier. A leader must fight this pressure with perseverance in order to insure completion.

1	2	3	4	5	6	7	8	9	10

Needs Improvement   *Excellent*

Comments and Growth Step Suggestions:

_____

_____

_____

Honesty

When a leader displays honesty, they are truthful and sincere, even in moments where it does not benefit the leader. Leaders who are honest are free from deceit or fraud. Honesty takes courage and commitment. When leaders are honest with themselves and their followers, growth will happen. True evaluation never happens outside of honesty.

1	2	3	4	5	6	7	8	9	10

Needs Improvement   *Excellent*

Comments and Growth Step Suggestions:

_____

_____

_____

Based on the results of this assessment, in what leadership character trait are you the strongest? In what trait do you need the most improvement?

Growth Steps

How can you grow in the character trait where you need the most improvement? (Suggestions: find someone older than you who exemplifies that trait and ask them to mentor you. Put yourself in a position where you need to exercise that trait more often. Ask a friend to keep you accountable in living out that trait. Take a look at the action step for that trait, and apply it.)

Before You Move On

Take some time to enter the results of your Leadership Skills and Traits into your Leadership Profile on page 92 of your workbook. Make sure to share your results with another person you trust so that they can keep you accountable for growing in your newly found knowledge of the Balancing Act. Remember, everything you learn about leadership is only valuable if you apply it in life.

SMALL GROUP STUDY TIME TABLE

Below is a table outlining the content of this session along with an approximate time-frame, which you can adapt to meet the needs of your group. Please take notice that several items should be prepared by students before coming to the small group so as to maximize time.

Session Outline	Description	Approximate Time-frame
Balancing Act	An examination of the 5 Leadership Skills and 5 Leadership Traits. Discuss with group.	*15 minutes*
Bible on Balancing Act	An in-depth and interactive look at the life of Nehemiah. Answer questions with group.	*15 minutes*
Leadership Skills	Scenario for students to develop and use their leadership skills.	*20 minutes*
Life Application	Questions evaluating the use of leadership skills.	*10 minutes*
Leadership Character Traits Assessment	Students should have self, parent, and youth worker assessment completed before hand. Complete peer assessment and discuss with group.	*Completed Before Small Group/15 minutes*
Life Application	Questions diving into how the group is living out leadership traits.	*10 minutes*
Group Activity	Divide group into pairs to share specific action plans (see below).	*10 minutes*

Group Activity

Divide the group into pairs and have them share their specific Growth Steps for how they will use their leadership skills and traits in the next week. Use the following questions for making applications:

- What are you going to do?
- Where are you going to do it?
- When are you going to do it?

Have each pair record their partner's application and then commit to praying for their partner and asking them at least once over the next week if they have accomplished their application goal.

MISSION FIRST: PEOPLE ALWAYS

SOME OF the world's greatest athletes have lost because they were disqualified for bad sportsmanship. At some point, they started caring more about winning than people. In leadership we must be aware of the same thing: the danger of caring more about the mission than our team. We call this Mission First: People Always. The concept seems easy when you first look at it, but living it out is extremely hard when you are in leadership. When dealing with the tasks in front of us and the relationships we build on the teams we lead, everyone ends up leading out of a particular style. This leadership style will generally favor one over the other, either valuing tasks more than relationships or vice versa. But in order for great leadership to occur, we must find an equal value for both the tasks and the relationships we encounter in leadership.

God has given us all a mission and that mission is to change the world. At the end of Jesus' time on Earth, he gathered his disciples together one last time and gave them a clear direction for their ministry after his departure:

> *Then Jesus came to them and said, "All authority in heaven and on earth has been given to me. Therefore go and make disciples of all nations, baptizing them in the name of the Father and of the Son and of the Holy Spirit, and teaching them to obey everything I have commanded you. And surely I am with you always, to the very end of the age."*
> *— Matthew 28:18–20*

Christ's last words became our mission here on this planet. It's known as the Great Commission and it's a call to all believers to impact the world in Christ's name. Within this greater mission, Jesus has crafted an individual plan for how he wants you to lead. Isn't this exciting? God has given you a personal mission for bringing the Kingdom of Heaven down to Earth. Our job on this planet—the whole changing the world thing—revolves around changing people's hearts and minds by introducing them to Christ. Through relationship with him, broken hearts are healed, families are restored, hatred is silenced, and peace rules our lives. Our purpose is people, and to that end, our leadership must reflect that truth.

In leadership, tasks and relationships are tied together. If our mission from God is reaching out to people, then we must also care for the people who accompany us on the mission road. Our tasks in the short run of accomplishing the mission may be fulfilled without necessarily caring for our followers, but at what cost? If the relationships are sacrificed, the task means nothing. Likewise, if greater emphasis is placed on relationships rather than tasks, meaningful friendships will form, but nothing will ever be accomplished. The concern for the task must equal the concern for relationships. If imbalance is present, your mission will eventually fail.

The Bible on Mission First: People Always

Below are multiple verses from both the Old Testament and the New Testament that touch on Mission First: People Always. Read through the verses below and point out specific statements that deal with mission and people. Circle statements that are mission oriented; underline statements that are people oriented.

And David shepherded them with integrity of heart;
with skillful hands he led them.
— Psalm 78:72

Let us not become weary in doing good, for at the proper time we will reap a harvest if we do not give up. Therefore, as we have opportunity, let us do good to all people, especially to those who belong to the family of believers.
— Galatians 6:9–10

Better a small serving of vegetables where there is love
than a fattened calf with hatred.
— Proverbs 15:17

We hear that some among you are idle and disruptive. They are not busy; they are busybodies. Such people we command and urge in the Lord Jesus Christ to settle down and earn the food they eat. And as for you, brothers and sisters, never tire of doing what is good.
— 2 Thessalonians 3:11–13

Make every effort to live in peace with everyone and to be holy; without holiness no one will see the Lord.
— Hebrews 12:14

Not that I have already obtained all this, or have already arrived at my goal, but I press on to take hold of that for which Christ Jesus took hold of me. Brothers and sisters, I do not consider myself yet to have taken hold of it. But one thing I do: Forgetting what is behind and straining toward what is ahead, I press on toward the goal to win the prize for which God has called me heavenward in Christ Jesus.
— Philippians 3:12–14

Live in harmony with one another. Do not be proud, but be willing to associate with people of low position. Do not be conceited.
— Romans 12:16

Commit to the LORD whatever you do,
and your plans will succeed. — Proverbs 16:3

For this reason I remind you to fan into flame the gift of God, which is in you through the laying on of my hands. For the Spirit God gave us does not make us timid, but gives us power, love and self-discipline.
— *2 Timothy 1:6–7*

Therefore, since we are surrounded by such a great cloud of witnesses, let us throw off everything that hinders and the sin that so easily entangles, and let us run with perseverance the race marked out for us.
— *Hebrews 12:1*

Bear with each other and forgive one another if any of you has a grievance against someone. Forgive as the Lord forgave you.
— *Colossians 3:13*

Be sure you know the condition of your flocks,
    give careful attention to your herds;
— *Proverbs 27:23*

Keep on loving each other as brothers and sisters. Do not forget to show hospitality to strangers, for by so doing some people have shown hospitality to angels without knowing it.
— *Hebrews 13:1–2*

And now these three remain: faith, hope and love. But the greatest of these is love.
— *1 Corinthians 13:13*

Now we ask you, brothers and sisters, to acknowledge those who work hard among you, who care for you in the Lord and who admonish you. Hold them in the highest regard in love because of their work. Live in peace with each other. And we urge you, brothers and sisters, warn those who are idle and disruptive, encourage the disheartened, help the weak, be patient with everyone.
— *1 Thessalonians 5:12–14*

What mission-oriented statement stuck out the most to you? Why?

_____

_____

_____

What people-oriented statement stuck out the most to you? Why?

_____

_____

_____

Did any specific verse challenge your thinking in any way?

_____

_____

_____

Mission First: People Always and You

It can be tough to envision exactly what it looks like when leaders value mission over people or vice versa. So, imagine for a moment that your youth group is on a one-week mission trip to an inner city location. You are partnering with a local ministry that provides neighborhood students assistance with tutoring and after school programs.

Each day, the center opens its doors to about 150 students, all who live in the neighborhood. Students from age 6 to age 18 receive help with their homework, play basketball in the gym, or learn new computer skills. The ministry also has ongoing Bible Clubs that challenge the students to think about their faith. They provide a valuable service to the community by keeping students off the dangerous, drug-infested streets and helping them graduate and go onto college. The center has actually assisted over 90% of its students in graduating high school and has sent about 60% on to college. Pretty remarkable considering the local graduation rate is only about 40%.

In spite of all this success though, the ministry still struggles to receive funding and has had to forego many needed repairs to their facility in order to pay for programming costs. Fortunately several groups, including yours, have agreed to partner with them and provide assistance in repairing the building throughout the next year. Your group of 27 students and 6 adult staff has been tasked with the responsibility of painting much of the facility, building an outside fence, and constructing shelves in several storage rooms. Your group will also be running a Vacation Bible School (VBS) for the younger kids in the program.

Your youth pastor decided months ago to give the responsibility of leading this trip over to the students and selected two main students to head up all the efforts. The two student leaders (we'll call them Brad and Gretchen) couldn't be more different. Both are strong leaders, but in different ways.

Brad is all about getting the job done. He's incredibly responsible and very hardworking, especially when it comes to doing work with his hands. He also loves managing a worksite, getting his opinions in whenever he can. Brad looks at the contributions from the team on the worksite as the most important part of the trip. So far on the trip, Brad thinks he's been doing really well, especially since the team is halfway done with all the work by the end of the second day. However he's been working his team into the ground and it's starting to wear on them. Brad seldom stops to talk to any of them, let alone encourage anyone on his team, and has yet to actually have a meaningful conversation with anyone from the ministry. In fact, Brad hasn't even participated at all during the VBS component of the trip. Everyone on the team believes Brad doesn't like them and are beginning to falter in their trust for him. When Brad tries to motivate them to finish strong on the work project, they've begun to just roll their eyes.

Gretchen is all about building relationships. She loves connecting with her team and has had a blast getting to know the ministry staff and students. Each day she has done a great job of asking tons of questions of her team, encouraging them to open up with her about their lives, dreams, and fears. Gretchen has also been incredible in VBS, submitting amazing ideas and infusing a level of enthusiasm into her peers that is unbelievable. Because of her efforts in these areas, the whole team feels a deeper connection with each other and with the kids in the ministry. Unfortunately, Gretchen can at times lose track of the task in front of her and in many situations has actually caused a delay in key moments of the worksite projects. This morning, her small group was supposed to cook breakfast, but had stayed up really late last night talking and overslept. Their delay made the whole team late in picking up the kids for VBS, and left many of the kids just waiting outside. Not to mention the time two days ago that Gretchen's group should have finished painting an outside wall, but were unable to finish. The deep questions Gretchen was asking seemed to stop all the work and an afternoon rainstorm came through the area, pushing all the students inside.

Both Brad and Gretchen are good leaders, but by no means are they great. Midway through this trip both of their leadership styles are beginning to not only show themselves, but also take away from the potential the trip could have. Take some time to answer the questions below about their styles of leading and what it means for their team.

What are the advantages of Brad's leadership style? Gretchen's?

_____

_____

_____

In each leadership style, what are they missing?

_____

_____

_____

Which leader do you think you resemble more: Gretchen or Brad? Why?

_____

_____

_____

Leadership Style Assessment

Tasks and relationships are hard to maintain equally when leading, but it is critical that a balance is maintained. Many leaders, however, look to lead out of only one, either holding up a greater importance for the task or for the relationships within a team. As a leader you may have a greater strength in one area over the other, but you must seek to value both at the same level or else your leadership will fail. If an unequal amount of value is distributed in these areas, you will either fail at accomplishing the task in front of you or your relationships will falter and dissolve. Both have happened to multiple leaders and you must be aware of your tendency to favor one over the other.

While the Leadership Wiring Assessment and the Spiritual Gifts Assessment were developed to help you discover what kind of a leader you are, the Leadership Style Assessment was created to help you discover how you lead when it comes to tasks versus relationships. This assessment will examine the link between your value for the tasks in front of you and your value for the relationships on your team. Knowing exactly what your tendencies are will help you determine how to better lead.

As with any assessment, your results will only be as accurate as the answers you give. Be sure to answer based on who you are really are, not who you would like to be or who others think you ought to be.

Scoring Guide

On the next pages are statements about leadership. Rate each one on a scale of 0–5 according to how closely the statement describes you. Please circle your answer.

	When leading a team...	Not at all like me				Very much like me	
1.	I keep close track of the schedule and deadlines	0	1	2	3	4	5
2.	I can take a big group and help people get to know each other	0	1	2	3	4	5
3.	I want to make sure the job is done right	0	1	2	3	4	5
4.	I like to write notes to encourage team members	0	1	2	3	4	5
5.	I like to focus on the work to be done	0	1	2	3	4	5
6.	I will often ask individuals if they have ideas to work more efficiently	0	1	2	3	4	5
7.	I like it when the group has strong relationships	0	1	2	3	4	5
8.	I'm good at solving technical problems	0	1	2	3	4	5
9.	I want to get to know the people I'm working with	0	1	2	3	4	5
10.	I demand that the team achieves the goal	0	1	2	3	4	5
11.	It's natural for me to encourage someone who is feeling down	0	1	2	3	4	5
12.	I like hanging out with the team	0	1	2	3	4	5
13.	I enjoy accomplishing the goal	0	1	2	3	4	5
14.	I am constantly looking for ways to improve relationships on the team	0	1	2	3	4	5
15.	I pay close attention to the quality of work being done	0	1	2	3	4	5
16.	I want my team to have a good time together	0	1	2	3	4	5
17.	I appreciate people who work hard	0	1	2	3	4	5
18.	I am concerned about getting the job done	0	1	2	3	4	5
19.	It bothers me when team members ignore each other	0	1	2	3	4	5
20.	The task to be accomplished is highly important to me	0	1	2	3	4	5
21.	I enjoy getting to know other people	0	1	2	3	4	5
22.	I like to write goals, schedules, and checklists	0	1	2	3	4	5
23.	I demand that people treat each other well	0	1	2	3	4	5
24.	Getting along with the others gives me a good feeling	0	1	2	3	4	5
25.	It's natural for me to teach someone how to do something	0	1	2	3	4	5
26.	I like it when the group gets a lot done	0	1	2	3	4	5
27.	I'm good at solving people problems	0	1	2	3	4	5
28.	I like planning the work to be done	0	1	2	3	4	5
29.	I will often ask individuals how they are doing personally	0	1	2	3	4	5
30.	I want my team to work together to win	0	1	2	3	4	5
31.	I pay close attention to the needs of the team members	0	1	2	3	4	5
32.	I keep close track of relationships on the team	0	1	2	3	4	5
33.	I appreciate people who are considerate of others	0	1	2	3	4	5

When leading a team...	Not at all like me				Very much like me	
34. Getting the job done right gives me a good feeling	0	1	2	3	4	5
35. The people under my care are highly important to me	0	1	2	3	4	5
36. I can take a big project and divide it into tasks and steps	0	1	2	3	4	5
37. I am concerned about what people need	0	1	2	3	4	5
38. It bothers me when team members talk instead of work	0	1	2	3	4	5
39. I am constantly looking for ways to improve the process of the team	0	1	2	3	4	5
40. I like to focus on the people doing the work	0	1	2	3	4	5

Now take your scores and transfer them to the appropriate column. Note that the numbers are not in consecutive order.

	TASK	RELATIONSHIP
	1._____	2._____
	3._____	4._____
	5._____	7._____
	6._____	9._____
	8._____	11._____
	10._____	12._____
	13._____	14._____
	15._____	16._____
	17._____	19._____
	18._____	21._____
	20._____	23._____
	22._____	24._____
	25._____	27._____
	26._____	29._____
	28._____	31._____
	30._____	32._____
	34._____	33._____
	36._____	35._____
	38._____	37._____
	39._____	40._____
Total	_____	_____

After you transfer your answers to the response sheet, use your answers to complete this grid. Plot your scores on the leadership style grid. First mark your task score on the horizontal axis, and then mark your relational score on the vertical axis.

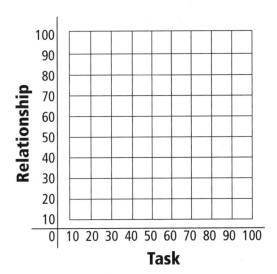

Leadership Zones

Your score will fall in or near one of five zones. Those who score high on relationships are relational leaders. Those who score high on tasks are task-oriented leaders. Those who score high on both dimensions are adaptive leaders. Those who score moderately on both are balanced leaders. Those who score low on both dimensions are inactive leaders. Adaptive leaders are the most effective over time and across a wide variety of settings. Inactive leaders are the least effective. Let's take a closer look at each of the five zones.

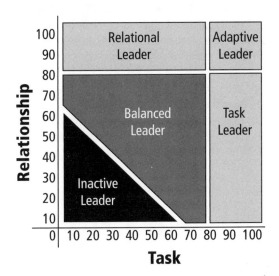

Mark your score on this grid. Your score will be in or near one of these five zones. Page 86 explains what each zone means.

Growth Strategies

Now that you have scored yourself on the task and relationship dimensions and located your score on the grid, you will want to know more about the two dimensions. Note that you can learn and grow in each of these dimensions which will improve your score and your overall leadership potential.

Tasks and Relationships

The questions in this profile indicate to what degree you are task-oriented as opposed to relationship-oriented. Those who are very task-oriented tend to focus on the work to be done, goals of the team, completing projects, and doing things the right way. They may focus on the tasks so much that they neglect or ignore the team members who are actually doing the work. Similarly, those who are very relationship-oriented tend to focus on the needs of team members, building relationships, and group cohesion. They may focus on people and relationships so much that they neglect the goal of the team or the work to be done. Some people are naturally more task-oriented and others are naturally more relationship-oriented. Some score high on both scales showing they are both task-oriented and relationship-oriented.

The most fundamental dynamic for leaders is learning how to balance concern for the task with concern for relationships. If leaders focus exclusively on the tasks, they may have unhappy team members or find their team falling apart. If leaders focus exclusively on relationships, they may find their team failing to achieve goals or getting enough work accomplished. A concern for the task and a concern for relationships are needed for any team to function at a high level.

At times, the leader will have to put more effort into building team relationships rather than pushing for the work to be done. At other times, the leader will have to focus on the work process more than the needs and desires of the team members. A good leader is able to provide what the team needs when the team needs it.

This means that leaders need to have a dual focus. Leadership is a balancing act of caring for goals to be achieved and also for the relationships to be maintained. Almost everyone can learn to do better at balancing concern for tasks with concern for relationships.

Leadership Zone Definitions

Adaptive Leaders (Very High Task / Very High Relationship)

Leaders in this zone score very high in both tasks and relationships. They are equally concerned about accomplishing the goal and taking care of the people. They are careful not to neglect either side. If the team is falling behind on the schedule, they emphasize the work to be done. If relationships are becoming frazzled, they take time out to resolve conflicts and encourage individuals.

Compare this leadership style to an outstanding football, baseball, or soccer coach who cares for players but also wants to win. The coach is concerned for each player individually and for the cohesiveness of the team as a whole. He or she is insistent on winning and finds ways to bring the best out of the team. The coach balances concern for winning with concern for the players. The coach wants both and settles for nothing less. He or she actively adapts and puts extra leadership effort on the task side or relationship side as needed.

Balanced Leaders (High Task / High Relationship)

Leaders in this zone score moderately high in both tasks and relationships. They tend to be sensitive to both the work to be done and the people doing the work. They are like adaptive leaders but not as intense. They get along with people and get the job done. They are concerned about accomplishing the task, but not as much as a task leader. They are concerned about people, but not as strongly as a relational leader. Team members generally like balanced leaders but can sometimes be disappointed by them.

Compare this leadership style to the sponsor of a school club. Whether working with the chess club, debate team, or yearbook staff, the teacher serving as sponsor is usually more relaxed than when teaching a class. He or she is warm towards the students and keeps the group on course. The teacher is well-liked and the projects get done.

Relational Leaders (Low Task / High Relationship)

Leaders in this zone score high in relationships but lower in tasks. They tend to be attuned to the quality of relationships on the team and the needs of individual team members. They want their team to be cohesive and comfortable. They want people to get along. They also tend to be less sensitive to times when the group needs structure and direction. Sometimes team members may become impatient if the group doesn't know what to do or isn't getting the work done on time.

Compare this leadership style to a caring counselor who is concerned for each person in the group as an individual as well as paying attention to the dynamics of the group as a whole. The group members feel listened to and cared for as individuals. They get to know each other on a deeper level and experience friendship and personal growth. The leader continually monitors the atmosphere in the group and spends time with individuals as necessary.

Task Leaders *(High Task / Low Relationship)*

Leaders in this zone score high in tasks but lower in relationships. They tend to keep their eye on the goal and the work to be done. They know how to provide structure for the group. They are good at planning and providing direction. They also tend to be less sensitive to the needs of the people on the team and as a result the quality of relationships on the team may suffer. Some team members may become so dissatisfied that they leave.

Compare this leadership style to a director of a play, band, or orchestra. The director demands the best out of the performers, working them for long hours and insisting on excellence. The director may spend no time afterwards with the performers. He or she may not even know everybody's name. The performers also may not get along very well as a group. But on stage, the director leads the group to deliver a brilliant performance.

Inactive Leaders *(Low Task / Low Relationship)*

Leaders in this zone score low in both tasks and relationships. They tend to be unaware of times when the group needs task direction and when it needs relational maintenance. When they do see a need, they either ignore it or respond way too late. They can appear distant, aloof, or uncaring. Those with the lowest scores tend to be ineffective in most any leadership situation. Inactive leaders can improve their leadership awareness and skills, but often they see no need.

Compare this leadership style to a teacher who gets stuck with a class he or she doesn't like and a subject matter outside of his or her interests. The teacher will resent the students. He or she will tend to be boring, uncaring, and low-energy when teaching. The students won't test well at the end of the semester and probably won't enjoy being together in the class.

Leadership Style Summary Chart

Relationship **(High)**	**Relational Leader** • wants to be your friend • wants you to have a good time • doesn't want to hurt your feelings • concerned with group atmosphere • unconcerned about performance • lets you decide *At best when:* • building relationships is the goal • leading a small group • in primarily social situations *Should beware of:* • wanting to be everyone's friend • neglecting the task or goal • being late or behind schedule • being too lenient	**Adaptive Leader and** **Balanced Leader** • wants the team to perform • wants team camaraderie • wants to accomplish the goal • wants the group to function well • concerned for task and relationship • decides together with you *At best when:* • leading high-performance teams • people want to grow • skilled leadership is needed *Should beware of:* • asking too much from people • taking on too much • neglecting tasks or relationships thinking that minimal effort is enough if balanced
(Low)	**Inactive Leader** • wants to be left alone • wants to be comfortable • unconcerned about you • unconcerned about the goal • concerned more about self • stalls on decisions *At best when:* • minimal leadership is required • group can easily succeed without the leader • ineffective in most situations *Should beware of:* • wanting to take it easy • neglecting the team goal or purpose • neglecting team members	**Task Leader** • wants to get the job done • wants you to follow • gives orders • concerned about succeeding • unconcerned about feelings • decides for you *At best when:* • team relationships are already strong • people don't know what to do • dealing with an emergency *Should beware of:* • being too pushy and demanding • neglecting team relationships • being oblivious to needs of people
	(Low) **Task** **(High)**	

How does your leadership style benefit you in leadership?
How could your leadership style hurt your leadership?

Growth Steps
In what specific ways can you be more effective in your leadership style?

Before You Move On
Take some time to enter your results from the Leadership Style Assessment into your
Leadership Profile on page 92 of your workbook. Make sure to share your results of
this assessment with another person you trust so that they can keep you accountable
for growing in your newly found knowledge of Mission First: People Always. Remember,
everything you learn about leadership is only valuable if you apply it in life.

SMALL GROUP STUDY TIME TABLE

Below is a table outlining the content of this session along with an approximate time-frame, which you can adapt to meet the needs of your group. Please take notice that several items should be prepared by students before coming to the small group so as to maximize time.

Session Outline	Description	Approximate Time-frame
Mission First: People Always	An examination of the Mission First: People Always principle. Read and discuss with group.	*10 minutes*
Bible on Mission First: People Always	An examination of this principle throughout scripture. Read and discuss with group.	*15 minutes*
Mission First: People Always and You	Scenario for students to examine different styles of leadership.	*15 minutes*
Leadership Style Assessment	Self assessment looking at students' style of leading. Discuss results of assessment with group.	*Completed Before Small Group/15 minutes*
Life Application	Questions diving into how leadership style affects the team.	*10 minutes*
Group Activity	Divide group into pairs to share specific action plans (see below).	*10 minutes*

Group Activity

Divide the group into pairs and have them share their specific Growth Steps for how they will use their leadership style in the next week. Use the following questions for making applications:

- What are you going to do?
- Where are you going to do it?
- When are you going to do it?

Have each pair record their partner's application and then commit to praying for their partner and asking them at least once over the next week if they have accomplished their application goal.

Leadership Profile

		My tendencies are...	I need to improve by...	Growth steps...
LEADERSHIP WIRING	Primary type: Supporting type:			
SPIRITUAL GIFTS	Primary gift: Supporting gift:	My typical strengths are...	My potential pitfalls are...	Growth steps...
LEADERSHIP SKILLS	Determine scope Calculate resources Cast the vision Navigate obstacles Evaluate performance	Strongest skill...	Skill I need to work on most...	Growth steps...
LEADERSHIP CHARACTER TRAITS	Vision Wisdom Enthusiasm Perseverence Honesty	Strongest character trait...	Trait I need to work on most...	Growth steps...
LEADERSHIP STYLE	Relationship score: Task score: Leadership Zone:	Leadership zone strengths...	Areas I need to improve on...	Growth steps...

Now what?

Congratulations! You have successfully completed *Student Leaders Start Here*. By going through this workbook you've discovered your leadership wiring and spiritual gifts (Leadership Design), come to understand the balance between leadership skills and character traits (The Balancing Act), and developed an equal value for tasks and relationships (Mission First: People Always). You have gained not only a deeper understanding of your own leadership, but hopefully you've also set in place action steps to improve your leadership. Yet this is only the beginning.

With everything you have learned about yourself, it's a great start for your long-term success in leadership. Now your job is to take your leadership past this workbook and into the world. How will you contribute to your youth group, your church, or local community? Just as the writer of Hebrews desired believers to leave behind the milk of their spiritual growth and move onto solid food, so you must also seek to challenge yourself by growing and maturing in your leadership. The information is within you for the beginning in leadership. It's now up to you to use it. You've officially stepped over the starting line and are running the race. Where will you lead the followers who run alongside you?

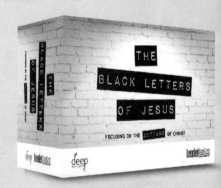